Narrowboat Planning

Designing the Interior of Your Boat

Graham Booth

Waterways World
Burton-on-Trent

Published by Waterways World Ltd
151 Station Street, Burton-on-Trent
Staffordshire DE14 1BG, England

Tel: 01283 742950
email: admin@wwonline.co.uk

ISBN: 1 870002 94 6

Based upon the series 'Going to Plan' published in *Waterways World* magazine

A catalogue record for this book is available from the British Library

Printed and bound in the United Kingdom by Information Press, Oxford

Other books by Graham Booth published by Waterways World Ltd

The Narrowboat Builder's Book:
The Complete Guide to Fitting Out a Narrowboat, 3rd edition

The Inland Boat Owners' Book, 3rd edition

Contents

Appendices

Part I

Welcome to *Narrowboat Planning*. In a sister volume, *The Narrowboat Builder's Book*, there is a section on the planning of my own boat, *Rome*, and some other options, so why produce a whole book on the subject?

The reason is two-fold. First, getting the plan right is one of the most important aspects of commissioning or fitting out a boat. In the many conversations I have with prospective boat buyers and DIY fitters, it is apparent that while some people can juggle spaces in their mind and visualise the final result perfectly, others have great difficulty in deciding what they want and then putting it down on paper. Even with the beds an impossible 4ft long, the overall length of the boat is often 100ft in length! The other is that after several years of reviewing and photographing boats, I have a good idea of what planning solutions are possible – and a record of how the finished result looks.

This book is therefore divided into two parts. This first part deals with some general principles of planning and takes a look at the design of the individual spaces usually found on a narrowboat. There are also some thoughts on the design of the fixed furniture that goes into these spaces and a chart giving the sizes of items often used in narrowboats. In Part 2 there are plans and photographs of boats of different lengths and types that are representative of the many basic approaches to planning.

This is not intended to be a marine version of the well known 'Plan-a home' book of house plans, although it could be used in that way. I would rather hope that it is a springboard to help you commission or build the boat that best suits your needs.

Graham Booth
April 2005

Chapter 1

Back to Basics

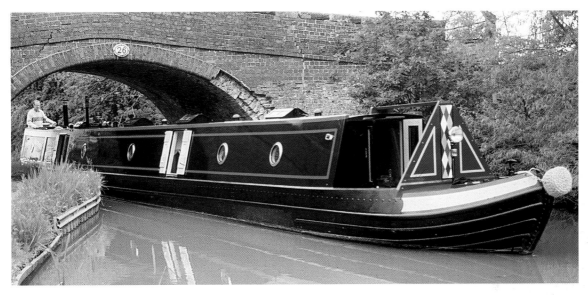

The size and shape of narrowboats are governed by the dimensions of the structures through which they pass

Like many types of inland craft, the size and shape of narrowboats are governed by the dimensions of the structures through which they pass as they make their way around the country. The maximum length and width are determined by the locks which, on the majority of the system, will accept a boat that is 70ft long and a nominal 7ft wide. However, on several of the northern canals, the locks are wider, but reduced in length, so that the maximum length of boat that can pass through is 57ft 6in.

The vertical dimensions of narrowboats are governed by the typical depth of the canals and the height above water level of the lowest bridge. These generally result in a draught of between 1ft 9in and 2ft 6in and an air draught (the height of the cabin above water level) of around 5ft 6in. By the time the hull is insulated and lined, the maximum internal

width below the gunwales is about 6ft 3in and the headroom is between 6ft 2in and 6ft 5in.

These constraints result in a narrow, tube-like boat in which the individual spaces are generally arranged one after the other rather than side by side or one above the other. You might think that this would result in a limited number of rather uninteresting layouts but, with a bit of imagination and ingenuity, it's amazing what can be achieved.

The only real choice you have as far as overall dimensions are concerned is whether to go for the maximum length and, if not, where to draw the line. To decide on this, you need to start by thinking about your likely cruising range. If you want to explore the whole system comfortably, you will have to limit yourself to an overall length of 57ft 6in. On the other hand, if you are happy to spend all your time on the canals and rivers of the Midlands and south, you could go to the full 70ft and enjoy much more room on the boat. But even though the thought of missing out on the Leeds & Liverpool or the Huddersfield Broad Canal may not worry you too much, you might still spare a thought for the effect that the inability to cruise these waters may have on the value of the boat when you eventually come to sell it.

There are, of course, other factors that could influence your decision. The costs of mooring and licensing a boat are determined by its length so, the longer you make it, the higher the annual running costs will be.

Typical
dimensions for
a narrowboat
cross section

5ft 4in to
5ft 8in

6ft 2in to
6ft 5in

6ft 8in to
7ft 0in

6ft 3in

1ft 10in

6ft 10in

The cost of the boat itself also depends on its length, although this is not quite so directly proportional. All boats, from the shortest to the longest, must have a bow, a stern, a galley, a loo and many other elements which are fairly constant in price. If you opt for a 55ft rather than a 45 ft boat, you are probably only adding 10ft of straight steel work and lining and some relatively inexpensive fixed furniture. This means that longer boats usually cost less per foot than shorter ones.

But there are other advantages in having a longer boat. In the example above, the overall boat length is increased by 22% but, because the front and rear decks and the engine rooms are relatively constant in size, the cabin will be 33% longer, making the boat feel far more spacious.

If asked, after a few months, what they would change if they could start all over again, most owners of new boats say they wish they had made the boat several feet longer. Of course, it is possible to extend the boat once it is complete but at a much higher price so, if in doubt, add those few extra feet at the planning stage.

Finally, there is the question of how large a boat you can manage. This may seem the most important point but, in practice, it is probably the least important. Every time we have bought a new, bigger boat, we have approached the first cruise with trepidation only to find that we become totally used to the extra few feet after the first couple of miles.

Large, heavy boats require more effort if you need to move them on ropes but, in normal cruising, you should not have to do this too often. Provided there is a centre rope, it is just as easy for one person to hold a 60ft boat while waiting at a lock as it is a fifty footer and, if pulling the boat into the bank is likely

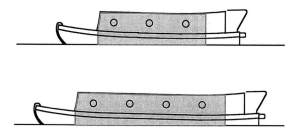

The 55ft boat (bottom) has 33% more useable cabin than the 45 footer (top) but is only 22% longer

to be a particular problem, you could consider installing a bow thruster. On the plus side, a heavier boat will generally stay where it is put in situations where a lighter boat is affected by side winds and cross currents.

Types of Shell

There are three basic types of narrowboat shell, and the main differences occur at the stern.

Traditional

'Traditional' sterns have small rear decks and upswept cabins modelled on their working boat ancestors. The engine is usually just inside the rear doors or, if the boat is really traditional, it has its own engine room ahead of a replica boatman's cabin. Traditional narrowboats have great eye appeal which makes them more popular and therefore hold their price better. Their main drawback is that they have difficulty in accommodating more than two people on the rear deck so a sizeable front deck is a must if you have a large crew or plan to invite lots of visitors.

The elegant lines of a traditional stern

Cruiser

The cruiser stern has space for the whole crew

In the second main type, the cruiser stern, the rear deck is much larger and the engine is installed beneath it. It allows the whole crew, including the steerer, to enjoy the scenery together and the large, flat area is ideal for open-air meals. The very non-traditional shape of the stern has inspired some designers to rethink the shape of the front of the boat and several more modern interpretations have occurred over the years.

Semi-traditional

This traditional looking boat has an open cockpit

Inevitably, the pros and cons of traditional and cruiser sterns have led to a compromise solution, known as the semi-traditional rear deck. This is basically a cruiser deck but with the cabin sides extended on either side of it to give some shelter to the steerer and a more traditional appearance to the boat. Whether this combines the best or worst aspects of the other types is a matter of personal taste.

Three types? well, maybe four because you could opt for a hybrid traditional and semi traditional. This has a traditional stern with a very large sliding hatch which opens to reveal what is, in effect, a semi-traditional rear deck. A further sub-variation is to add a small hinged flap in the rear edge of the hatch so that the steerer's lower half can be protected from the elements as he or she would in a fully traditional boat.

The hinged flap in this large slide gives maximum flexibility

Two final caveats

Before we get into the more detailed aspects of boat planning, there are two very important things you should bear in mind. One of the advantages of commissioning a one-off boat or fitting it out yourself is that you can design it in a way that exactly suits your needs or expresses your personality. However, without wishing to dull your enthusiasm or creativity, it is worth remembering that you may want to sell the boat one day and the depreciation will be far greater if the layout or finishes are too radical.

The other concerns the shell. Almost regardless of what you or the boat fitter do to the inside, the boat will always be judged principally by the line and quality of the shell. A superb fit out in an indifferent shell will be a poor investment whereas a dull fit out in a quality shell can always be improved or even stripped out and re-done. Take your time and study the market to see whose shells look good and keep their value best when they are sold.

Chapter 2

Planning

Planning a narrowboat is not like baking a cake or assembling an MFI wardrobe – there are no step-by-step instructions for you to follow that will, hopefully, enable you to reach your goal. You have to have some idea of the overall plan before you can decide on the individual spaces, but you really need to know roughly how these spaces will be designed before you can start thinking about the plan. To overcome this 'Catch 22' situation, let's start by looking at some popular layouts to get a feel of what is involved and then, in the following chapters, examine the possibilities for planning the spaces within and the effects these have on the overall plan.

Medium and large boats

The most popular length of narrowboat is between 48ft and 57ft long and the most popular layout for boats of this length is what has become known as the 'floating cottage' plan. This is ideal for traditional or semi-traditional style boats intended for two adults and occasional guests. At the front of the boat is a saloon, which often has some form of seating that can be used for

dining and converts to an occasional double bed. Next comes the galley, followed by the bathroom, followed by the bedroom with a fixed double bed and then, finally, there is the engine room.

This basic layout may seem rather commonplace but that is largely because it has so many advantages. The saloon has easy access to the front deck which, on fine days, becomes an extension of the internal space. The galley is adjacent to the saloon which is also used for dining, the two sleeping areas are at opposite ends of the boat for maximum privacy and the bathroom is in between so that there is individual access for both at night.

If the boat is over 55ft, a few variations on this theme are possible. A dinette that converts to a double bed can be added between the galley and the saloon or, if it is longer than 60ft, between the bathroom and galley.

In a boat that is 60ft or over, a traditional back cabin, which contains additional sleeping accommodation, can be added beyond the engine space. The traditional back cabin option means that the engine is no longer in a semi-external compartment

Key to Plans	
S	Saloon
G	Galley
Bt	Bathroom
Bd	Bedroom
E	Engine room
Dn	Dinette
Bc	Back cabin

'Floating cottage' layout in a boat of 48–55 ft
– the front deck becomes an extension of the saloon

With a boat over 55ft long a dinette can be aded to the basic 'floating cottage' – here the dinette can be converted to a double bed at night

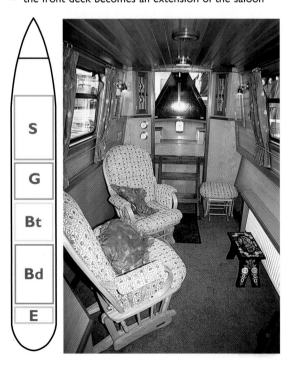

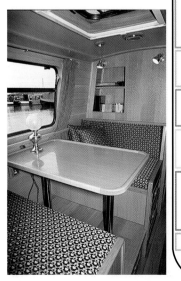

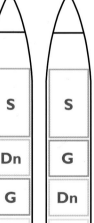

The 'floating cottage' plan can be reversed for a boat with a cruiser stern – the double doors in the saloon here open onto the rear deck rather than the front.

A boat of more than 60ft could use the extra length to add a boatman's cabin to the 'floating cottage' layout. Boatman's cabins have a great atmosphere as well as providing extra sleeping accommodation

An alternative plan for a cruiser-stern boat places the galley at the rear – this can act as a lobby

or hidden under a plywood casing that also serves as the steps to the rear deck. Instead, it has its own room where it can be boxed in but is normally allowed to sit in full splendour for all to see. This arrangement gives better access to the engine for servicing and provides a useful room for drying wet gear or storing small items. If the back cabin, rather than the dinette or saloon, is to be the second sleeping area, the bathroom is usually relocated between the main bedroom and the engine room so that individual access is maintained.

Traditional-style boats may be the most popular type with private boaters but they do not suit everyone. If you prefer a cruiser stern, you could still use the 'floating cottage' plan or you could reverse it so that the saloon is at the back of the boat. In this position, it is adjacent to the rear deck where all the action is likely to be.

Alternatively, the galley could be at the back followed by the saloon, bathroom and then the bedroom at the front. This allows the galley to act as a lobby where wet shoes and coats can be shed before entering the carpeted saloon, which makes it particularly popular with boaters who cruise right through the winter.

Having the bedroom at the front means that the front well deck can be smaller, or even eliminated altogether, and the space that is saved used elsewhere.

The small front doors of this forward bedroom are for escape

Shorter boats

Planning a larger narrowboat can be a problem, but planning a small one is a real test of ingenuity. When you are planning a boat of less than 35ft, some overlapping and double use of accommodation is inevitable. In this category, there are no standard solutions, so let's look briefly at three specific examples.

Our first narrowboat was 33ft long and had a 20ft cabin. We decided to have an L-shaped dinette/double bed occupying virtually all of the saloon at the front, a galley with a central corridor, followed by a long, thin bathroom on the port side and a fixed single berth on the starboard. This meant that we had to make and unmake the bed every day but we reckoned that the amount of day space which this gave us made it worthwhile. We might just have managed to squeeze in a fixed double bed at the back but this would have meant an even smaller bathroom, galley and saloon.

The layout of a narrowboat, just 33ft long

The 30ft Davison Short Boat of the late 1970s had two rear single berths whose foot ends went under the rear deck either side of the small boxed-in engine. There was a double berth/dinette at the front and a single berth/dinette opposite the galley, which gave it a total of 5 berths.

A few years later, the 31ft Brum Tug adopted a more radical solution by coupling a traditional back

Our first narrowboat was 33ft long – the whole interior could be seen through the front doors

cabin with various combinations of additional accommodation where the engine room would normally be. This provided layouts that were compact and full of character.

Circulation

It is possible to plan the boat so that there is no access from the rear deck into the cabin. As well as prolonging the life of the carpet, this makes the space at the back of the cabin – usually a bedroom or bathroom – feel much wider and more private. On the downside, it increases the steerer's isolation and some sort of hatch must be provided near the back of the main cabin for emergency escape. It also means that any passage from the front deck to the rear deck has to be via the side decks or the roof and, in some weather conditions, this may not be entirely safe.

Assuming that you opt for a route from the front to the rear

solid fuel stove – old fashioned warmth
decorated drop table
drop double bunk – home comfort
plenty of storage space
stainless sink/cooker unit
water heater
plank
forward hold, which can be covered to provide camping style accommodation for extra crew

quiet running 12hp water-cooled diesel engine
side bunk
not shown – generous self contained shower and toilet area
forward stable door and window
water tank and gas locker

The Brum Tug

A very wide and private bathroom at the back of the cabin

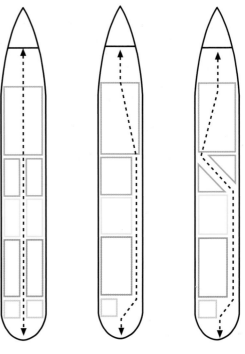

Mid corridor   Side corridor   Balanced corridor

Central corridors allow the maximum accommodation in the minimum cabin length, but can make the interior boring. With a side corridor your boat will require carefull ballasting. A balanced corridor layout can switch sides through the galley

deck through the cabin, you have the choice of locating it down the centre of the boat, to the port or starboard side, or a combination of all three.

Central corridors were very popular on hire boats as they allowed the maximum accommodation to be fitted into the minimum length of cabin. In present-day private boats, they are sometimes preferred by people who are exceptionally tall and need the extra headroom at the middle of the boat or by people who suffer back problems and need to be able to move about without twisting or leaning over. The disadvantages of central corridors are that it is not possible to have a fixed double bed or a reasonably sized, enclosed bathroom. They also allow you to see from one end of the boat to the other in one glance, which can make for a less interesting interior.

Many 'floating cottage' plans have a side corridor all the way through the boat, which is almost as boring and requires some careful ballasting if the boat is not to list to the side opposite the corridor when the fit out is complete.

The best solution is to vary the position of the corridor as it passes through the boat. This balanced approach means that ballasting is not so critical and views through the boat are more interesting because you cannot

see the whole of the interior as soon as you enter. One of the easiest places to switch the corridor from one side to the other is in the galley but it can be done in a through bathroom or even a midships bedroom with two single berths.

The galley is a good place to switch the corridor from one side to the other

Chapter 3

The Saloon

The saloon may seem an easy place to start but, in practice, it can be one of the most difficult to get right. It is the area where you will want to relax after a long day's locking or to entertain your friends so the main priority is to have sufficient comfortable seating. The saloon's size is often determined by subtracting the lengths of all the other, more dimensionally critical areas, like bedrooms and bathrooms, from the maximum length of boat you can fit into your mooring and seeing what is left. This may be unavoidable but, as we shall see, the size of the saloon has a strong influence on how you plan it. The two basic choices are whether you go for free-standing or built in seating.

Free-standing furniture

Free-standing furniture is nearly always more comfortable, which is why so many owners of residential boats opt for it. It does, however, take up slightly more space than built-in seating. Generously upholstered domestic settees are the worst culprits, often forcing their occupants to sit with their knees practically touching the wall opposite. If you decide to take this route, look for smaller pieces, low enough to tuck under the gunwale if possible, and try to restrict yourself to a compact two-seater settee that you can position across the boat or at an angle, rather than along it.

Chairs on legs or pedestals, which allow you to see the floor beneath, do not appear to take up as

Chairs on legs or pedestals appear to take up less space

much room as conventional armchairs that go right down to the floor. You could be lucky and find what you are looking for at the local furniture shop but you may do better to go to one of the firms specialising in chairs and settees designed for boats. Many of these can be converted to make occasional beds. To accommodate two armchairs, plus a cupboard, a stove and some bookshelves, the saloon should ideally be not less than 11ft long. If an additional settee is required, 15ft is about the minimum for comfort.

Room for dining

It is not always possible to have a separate dining area, so you may have to eat in the saloon. If you

A small settee positioned across the boat is not so overpowering

Four chairs fit into the base of this table

have enough space, you could have a small free-standing dining table and some proper dining chairs or maybe one of those clever drop-leaf tables that contain four folding chairs in the base.

Where space is more limited, you may have to resort to a drop leaf table or a table top on a Desmo* leg and use the easy chairs as dining chairs. In this case, you will need to ensure that the table is lower, or that the Desmo leg is shorter than usual, or your nose will be on the same level as the plate.

Another solution is to have fixed to the hull side a hinged flap that can be swung up and supported horizontally for dining.

Or, if you prefer a more traditional appearance, you could incorporate a boatman's cabin style table cupboard.

Above: A boatman's cabin style cupboard in the saloon could be used for dining

Below left and right: A lift-up flap forms a neat dining table

* A Desmo leg is a metal tube of about 2in diameter with slightly tapered ends. These ends fit into sockets let into the floor and screwed to the underside of a table top to form a table. If the table is large and oblong, two supports may be needed. The legs are available from chandlers in chrome or painted finish and in various lengths depending on the required height of the table. Extra sockets can be let into the floor so that the table can be used in various locations.

Built-in seating

Built-in seating is located right back against the hull side with no wasted space behind it. It has the advantage that the bases can be used for additional storage. The only drawback is that, unless you design it very carefully, the chances are that you will get a crick in your neck or pins and needles in your leg. The usual causes of this are seats that are too high and flat, back rests that are too upright and cushion foam that is the wrong density.

Measure the seat height of your lounge suite and you will probably find that it is a lot lower than you thought. Fifteen inches is about the norm, which means that allowing for a compressed 4in or 5in cushion, the fixed part should be no higher than about 12in although, if you or your crew are unusually tall or short, you may have to adjust this height slightly. The aim should be to have your knees just higher than your pelvis so that you tend to fall back into the seat and not forward off it. A thicker roll incorporated into the front edge of the seat cushion will distribute your weight more evenly along your thighs without having to resort to sloping the base of the seat. However, if the seating is to convert to a bed you will have to ensure that the rolls end up at the head and foot of the bed, leaving the middle part flat.

Backrest angle and the amount of lumbar support are dependant on personal taste but a back cushion resting against the near vertical hull side is generally too upright. An angle of around 10° to 12° from the vertical is about right. This can be achieved with a separate board which sometimes forms part of the base of an occasional bed.

The density of the foam is also partly a matter of taste but don't be fooled into thinking that very soft equals very comfortable. Foam is referred to by density in kg/cubic metre and hardness in Newtons. A 40/200 foam will give you a fairly firm support while a 40/135 foam is relatively soft, so you should find something that suits you in between these. Four

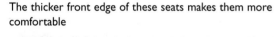

A typical built-in seat

The thicker front edge of these seats makes them more comfortable

Above: The backrest angle in this unit can be infinitely varied …

… until it finally becomes a bed (below)

inch thickness is usually adequate for seating although this could be increased to 4¹/₂in or 5in if it is to be regularly used as a bed as well. Whichever density you use, make sure it is the combustion modified type.

Access to the storage beneath built-in seating is usually by lift-off tops or drop-down fronts. Lifting the top makes it easier to get to things at the back but you have to move all the cushions first. Drop-down fronts give the opposite advantages/disadvantages. One way round this is to have large drawers mounted on castors or fridge rollers. These can be pulled out easily when required and let you get right to the back.

A popular form for built-in seating is an 'L' shape, which can be used for lounging or dining and, with a pull-out or lift-up insert, can become a double bed. In dining mode, the table is usually a loose piece supported on Desmo legs. It is possible to buy shorter Desmo legs and use the table top as part of the bed base, but it is more usual to extend the plywood top of the built-in base in some way.

The sloping backrest example described earlier shows one way this can be achieved but it can also be done by joining two pieces of plywood along the front edge with a piano hinge so that the top one can pivot through 180° and fill the gap (see diagram 1).

An L-shaped seating unit with a table top supported on Desmo legs

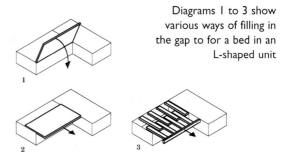

Diagrams 1 to 3 show various ways of filling in the gap to for a bed in an L-shaped unit

Another way is by sliding one piece over the other, although it is more difficult in this case to make both pieces level when they are in bed mode (see diagram 2). A neat, but more complicated, answer is to make the bases from softwood slats (which is also better for ventilation) so that they telescope together (see diagram 3).

The next problem is how to support the outer corner of the bed base. Possible solutions are a false door front that is hinged at the side and pivots out at right angles when needed (see diagram 4), or a pull-out panel, rather like the props you pull out to support the writing surface of a bureau (see diagram 5). For either of these methods, the outer edge of the base would have to have a reinforced long edge to stop it sagging. If you opt for the drawer solution for storage, the drawer can be used to support the insert along both edges and store the bedding as well (see diagram 6). Whatever you choose, the top should be at the right height to make the whole base level.

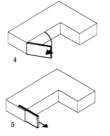

Diagrams 4 to 6 show how the bed insert can be supported

A more flexible alternative to the L-shaped unit is to have part of the seating built in and the other part moveable but made to the same dimensions. This enables you to arrange the units in different ways to suit your needs.

As the example below also shows, you can have some of the furniture produced by the builder and part of it bought in – but you may have to draw up a rota to decide who has the chair.

With built-in seating, you should be able to seat four people in reasonable comfort and leave space for occasional tables or stools and a stove in a saloon of about 12ft. However, if space is really tight, you could restrict the furniture to one L-shaped unit, in which case the saloon could be reduced to around 8ft.

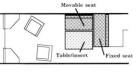

2/3 person dining

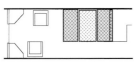

4 person dining

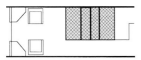

Guests sleeping

A dinette using both built-in and moveable seating can provide flexible dining/sleeping accommodation

A centrally located stove provides a strong focus

Other furniture

Whether a saloon has free-standing or built-in furniture, two items which appear either side of the front doors in many boats are a solid fuel stove and a triangular cupboard to house the television and possibly hi-fi. This is quite a good location for the television cupboard as it tends to reduce the amount of reflections from windows.

However, this is not such a good place for the solid fuel stove because its heat is only felt at one end of the boat. Moving the stove to the other end of the saloon where, in the floating cottage layout, it meets the galley, means that the heat will be spread more evenly throughout the boat. Also, if you opt for a stove with a back boiler and radiator system to spread the heat even further, the pipe runs will be shorter and it will be easier to get the upward slope on the pipes that is required to make the water circulate around the system without a pump.

In this situation, the stove is usually located against the side of the boat so that entry to the galley can be in the middle or on the opposite side of the plan. Alternatively, the stove can be on the centre line of the boat where it forms a strong focus for

A typical corner TV cupboard

the saloon. In this case, the entry to the galley can only be to one side or the other. Either way, you will not be able to position an L-shaped seating unit at the rear end of the saloon.

One area of the boat that is often ignored is the space under the gunwale. If you are lucky, you might be able to tuck the backrest of an armchair under there and gain a few extra inches of width but, on many boats, it is simply a place to hang a radiator. When you sit down in the evening, you are presented with a large expanse of boring plywood or carpet lining at eye level. This space is ideal for some shelves and cupboards to absorb the books and general clutter of modern living and, if built around the radiators, they will reduce the radiators' visual impact. Shelving and cupboards can also incorporate the lift up dining table mentioned earlier. Three or four inches may not seem very deep but it is amazing how much storage these units can provide.

Under gunwale shelves absorb a surprising amount of clutter

Chapter 4

The Galley

As an independent supply of 230-volt power becomes more common in modern narrowboats, many of the pieces of equipment found in a kitchen at home can be installed in the galley. Some of these items, like a dishwasher, may be desirable but are not essential so let's start by considering a galley equipped with the basic necessities which are a fridge, a sink and drainer unit and a cooker. These, together with the storage cupboards that make up the rest of the plan all sit conveniently into squares that are about 1ft 9in by 1ft 9in so these become the 'building blocks' of the galley.

In planning a domestic kitchen, the three basic elements are usually arranged in the sequence 'storage' i.e. the fridge, 'preparation' i.e. the

A through galley provides a compact solution on this 2-person boat

sink, and 'cooking' i.e. the cooker. These elements are also kept as near to one another as possible to minimise journeys between them but, in a narrowboat, there is rarely scope for these subtleties and, in any case, in such a relatively small space, everything is close to everything else.

What is more important is how the galley relates to the areas on either side of it. As well as being the place where the appointed cook spends much of their time, the galley is usually a through route. Whether it is approached from a side or central position has a large influence on how many building blocks can be accommodated in a given length, how accessible they are and how easy it is to get past the cook without incurring their displeasure.

Layout
Through galleys

Through galleys are entered, at both ends, from the centre of the plan. Because they have two unbroken lengths of worktop and storage units, through galleys manage to pack the most equipment and storage into the shortest length of boat. An average galley would have four

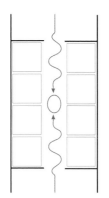

Through galley: 100% efficient

building blocks on either side of the corridor although this could be reduced to three, at a pinch. For the purpose of comparing one layout with another, let's assume that a four building block galley gives 100% efficiency.

Another advantage of through galleys is that they avoid those difficult-to-get-at corner cupboards. Their only drawback is that the cook has to work in the middle of what is effectively a narrow corridor and squeezing past can become a problem. Nevertheless, if space is tight and you only plan to have two or three people at a time on board, this type of plan is well worth considering.

U-shaped galleys

U-shaped galleys are approached from a corridor to one side and the units are laid out in a 'U' shape to the other side. Their pros and cons are the exact opposite of through galleys; there is less storage and they have two 'dead' corners but provide a safe refuge for the cook from the stampeding crew. Assuming the same length of galley as the example above, a

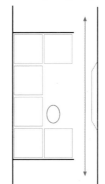

U-shaped galley: 75% to 80% efficient

A typical U-shaped galley

A lift-up flap adds worktop space in a thwartships galley

A flap across the corridor increases worktop space but limits passage through the boat

A hinged flap can also be positioned across one of the ways in to increase the amount of worktop space. This can be useful when cooking for a large number of people but it does make through traffic virtually impossible while it is in place.

U-shaped galley would contain six 'building blocks' so it would be only 75% efficient. It may be possible to add a shallow storage unit in the corridor, which would increase the efficiency to about 80%.

One way around the corner-unit problem can be found at kitchen specialists that sell useful devices like carousels and pull-out shelves for maximising storage in awkward spaces. Another way is to have a double door, hinged down the middle, which opens to reveal a larger opening so that you can see, and get to, what is at the back.

A double door gives better access to the 'dead' corner

A more radical solution to this problem is to dispense with the middle units altogether, leaving just the thwartships ones. Additional worktop space can be provided by a lift-up flap fixed to the hull side but this solution does have the obvious disadvantage of reducing the storage space still further.

L- shaped galleys

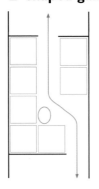

L-shaped galley: 87.5% efficient

In between the previous two contrasting plans are L-shaped and double L-shaped galleys. If your plan allows you to enter the galley from a central corridor but leave from one side, you could have an L-shaped worktop on one side and a slightly shorter straight run on the other. This has only one 'dead' corner and, depending on how long the straight run is, gives a reasonable amount of refuge space in the crook of the 'L'. It scores a middling 87.5% in the efficiency ratings. One drawback is that it will only work on galleys of about 7ft minimum length.

Double-L-shaped galleys

The double 'L' has opposing entry points, two dead corners once again and requires even more boat length for it to work. An increase in circulation space reduces its efficiency to 80%. Its main advantage is in making a more interesting overall boat plan by avoiding the continuous side corridor.

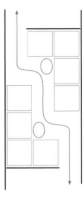

Double-L-shaped galley; 80% efficient

A double-L-shaped galley

Storage

In all layouts, the amount of storage can be increased by adding wall cupboards. Provided that they are not over-done, wall cupboards can add interest to the galley, but too many can make it feel claustrophobic. They can have concealed lighting fitted to the undersides which will put light just where it is needed on the worktop. One point to watch is forward-facing cupboards because, if you hit a lock gate, the doors can burst open and contents fly forward. If it is unavoidable, you could add fiddle rails to the shelves or fit strong bolts to the doors and make sure you remember to use them when cruising.

Another efficient way to increase storage space is also to be found at kitchen specialists. Floor-to-ceiling, sliding storage units can be housed in a cupboard off a side corridor and provide large amounts of easily accessible storage.

The corridor in a U-shaped galley can also be used for the type of under-gunwale cupboards described in the chapter on saloons. These are ideal for storing tins, bottles and cereal packets.

One place that is often ignored is in the base of the lower storage units. By raising the base board a touch and adding a drop-down front in place of the usual skirting, some useful storage space can be created. Since it is at the lowest level of the boat, this tends to stay quite cool so that vegetables and even butter and milk will survive for a reasonable time if stored there.

Equipment

The majority of narrowboats nowadays have a gas cooker and an electric fridge and these can be installed without creating any particular planning difficulties. It is advisable to have some worktop space on both sides of the cooker so that hot pans can be moved there in a hurry if necessary.

If you have concerns about having gas on board, a popular alternative is the diesel-fired stove. These take considerably longer than a gas stove to get up to temperature so many owners leave them ticking over between meals, which is fine in the spring or autumn but not so good on a hot summer's day. It is, therefore, a good idea to have a pair of side doors or a 'Houdini' roof hatch near to the stove to get rid of surplus heat in warm weather. Some larger stoves are

Proprietary sliding units provide efficient storage

This large diesel fired stove is centrally placed and has a 'Houdini' hatch nearby to allow the heat to escape

better located on the centre line of the boat where their weight does not affect the trim so much.

Another solution to the gasless-cooking problem is an electric oven and hob but these require 10 or 11 kW of power to allow unrestricted use. The only way to provide this is with a generator or with a PropGen package from Beta Marine. Both of these take up additional space, which must be taken into account when you plan the rear part of the boat.

Modern 12-volt electric fridges take remarkably little power from the batteries but, if you live aboard or want to stay for a few days in the places you visit, you may prefer one that uses no power at all. If you are one of the majority that is still happy to use gas, an LPG fridge can be installed but it must draw its combustion air, and emit its exhaust gases, directly to and from the outside air. This is achieved by having a small balanced flue terminal in the cabin side or the roof and this is connected to the fridge by flexible pipes housed in a ventilated casing. You will therefore need to allow for a full or part casing above the fridge. This will take up a small amount of worktop, although it could also provide a useful shelf.

This microwave can be hidden from view when not in use

sacrifice precious storage space. Another solution is to conceal the washing machine or tumble drier in cupboards in other parts of the boat or form a general purpose space at the rear. This can also be very useful as an area for hanging wet clothes and storing muddy boots or as a small, out-of-the-way study.

Washing machines can be tucked into the most unlikely places

The casing above this gas fridge provides an additional shelf

Beyond the minimum

If you are planning to spend a lot of time on your boat, you may be thinking of including a microwave, a freezer, a washing machine, a tumble drier and possibly even a dish washer. All of these are possible but they all take up space and, particularly in the case of the last two, consume quite a lot of power so, once again, you may also have to find room for a generator.

A microwave oven can be simply stood on a worktop but, since this space is usually at a premium, it is better to build the microwave into a range of cupboards. It can also have its own up-and-over door to shield it from view.

Larger pieces of equipment can be housed in the galley but you will either have to increase its size or

Freezers, which are used less frequently than a fridge, can also be located in a more remote place but you must ensure that there is adequate ventilation to the unit or it will not run efficiently.

Boundary Disputes

Assuming that the galley is somewhere in the middle of the boat, it has to butt up against the spaces on either side and the way it does this has an effect on the feel of the interior.

Looking rearwards, there is usually a bathroom or bedroom so the boundary is formed by a solid partition. Unlike the cabin and hull sides, this runs vertically from floor to ceiling so, in a U- or L-shaped galley, tall fittings like a high-level, built-in oven unit can be placed against it. This makes good practical sense and a microwave oven can usually be fitted in above, but it often means that the first thing that catches your eye when you enter the boat is the oven which, nine times out of ten, will have a drying cloth draped over the handle.

Centrally placed, high-level oven units make the worktop space between themselves and the side of

The worktop beside a centraly placed oven can only really be used for storage

A Welsh dresser has great eye appeal but needs fiddle rails to keep its contents in place

the boat virtually unusable. The best solution here is to extend the cupboards or shelves over this part or use it for storage.

Another possibility for the back wall is a Welsh dresser unit which has much more eye appeal but, for the reasons mentioned above, should have substantial fiddle rails.

At the other end of the galley, where it normally meets the saloon, the choices have even more impact. It is possible to have a solid partition here too and, if you are not the world's tidiest cook, this may be the option to go for. However, unless the saloon is quite large, or you are deliberately trying to create a 'cosy cottage' atmosphere, the interior will look more cramped than it otherwise would.

Taking the opposite approach and omitting the partition altogether makes the interior seem bigger but, especially in the case of a through galley, the lack of any sort of barrier can make it look as though you just ran out of galley units.

The 'middle way' approach of having what used to be called a room divider has much to commend it. Useful shelves or glass-doored cupboards can be supported on columns to form an open screen so that the cook can be a part of what is happening in the saloon but is able to retreat into the realms of gastronomy when required.

If free-standing furniture is used in the saloon, it is possible to incorporate a small door at the base of the screen to give access to a 'dead' corner in a U-shaped galley.

In a smaller boat, where even an open screen might be too overpowering, it is sufficient simply to have a low partition that stands about six inches above the worktop height. This could incorporate some useful shelves on the saloon side.

Open shelves give some privacy to the galley without isolating the cook

A small door gives access from the saloon to the 'dead' corner which, in this case, houses the water pumps

Chapter 5

The Bathroom

No matter how large or small your narrowboat is, you will need a room that contains, as a minimum, a toilet, a wash basin and either a bath or shower. These need to be installed in an area that is large enough to allow you to use them properly but not so large that it takes valuable space from other parts of the boat – a tall order.

In most cases, the bathroom will be somewhere in the middle of the boat so that the sleeping areas on either side can have independent access to it at night. In this position, the design has to allow you and your crew to pass from one end of the boat to the other during the daytime. This can be done either by creating an 'enclosed' bathroom with a corridor passing alongside it or a 'through' bathroom where the route goes through the bathroom itself. As with most alternative ways of planning the boat, there are plusses and minuses to each approach.

Layout
Enclosed bathrooms
The need to provide a corridor of at least 2ft in width means that the enclosed bathroom can only be about 4ft wide. At the same time, a desire to use as little of the boat's length as possible usually limits the length to about 6ft. This gives an area that is adequate but by no means generous. The compensating advantage is that, once you are installed and the door is locked, you can stay in there soaking your aching limbs for as long as you like without preventing the crew from moving around the rest of the boat.

The most popular and practical layout for an enclosed bathroom has a central circulation space

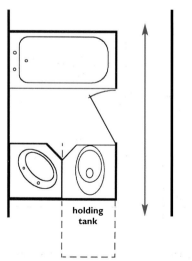

Typical layout of an enclosed bathroom

holding tank

with the washbasin and toilet to one side and the bath or shower to the other.

If the toilet is the dump-through type, fitted directly over the holding tank, it is better positioned towards the main corridor so that the tank is central in the boat and does not make it list to one side as it fills. To hold a reasonable amount of waste, the tank needs to be about 4ft long by 2ft wide by 1ft high, which makes it larger than the space immediately beneath the toilet. You should therefore ensure that whatever is on the other side of the partition can accommodate the remaining part.

Cassette toilets were designed originally for caravans where it is quite easy for the cassette to be discreetly removed from the base through a hatch in the outside wall. This is obviously not possible on a boat so a cassette toilet should also be positioned against the corridor wall in which a hatch can be provided.

Cassettes are removed through a hatch in the corridor wall and spares can be stored in the base of the vanity unit

Electric, vacuum and compression toilets discharge their waste to a holding tank, which can be located in virtually any part of the boat but is often under a fixed double bed.

The basin is usually against the hull where its use could be restricted by the inward slope of the cabin side. One way to give more elbow room is to place it at 45°.

The bath occupies the whole of the opposite side of the room but, if a shower is used, you can position the calorifier or a washing machine in the corner against the hull and build an airing cupboard around it which also forms the third wall of the shower cubicle.

20

Dump-through toilet against the corridor and a corner basin set at 45°

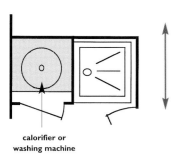

calorifier or washing machine

Replacing the bath with a shower makes space for the calorifier or a washing machine with an airing cupboard above

Though bathrooms allow you more scope to make a real style statement

Through bathrooms

By taking in the area of the corridor, through bathrooms are 50% bigger for any given length of bathroom so that there is plenty of room for wielding the biggest bath towel. The extra space also allows more flexibility in planning the room and, if you feel so inclined, more opportunity to make a real style statement. The pain that accompanies this particular gain is that anyone using the room for any length of time forces other members of the crew to use the towpath or gunwale to get from one end of the boat to the other. Another drawback is that, even when the bathroom is not occupied, people passing through the boat may be greeted by the sight of the loo, although this can sometimes be hidden behind an open door.

Depending on the layout of the areas either side, the doors into the bathroom can be from either side or the centre or a combination of the two although, in most cases, one door is to the side and the other is in the centre. As the following examples show, through bathrooms offer a greater number of planning options.

The bath can be placed across the boat, in which case it will still be restricted to a length of 4ft, or down the length of the boat which allows a full length bath

or a curved corner bath to be accommodated. Vanity units can be the corner type or a longer run of cupboards with a basin set in the top.

To ensure your privacy, you have to remember to lock both doors but it is possible to fit a device similar to the central locking system on a car which locks both doors simultaneously.

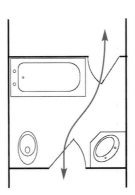

6ft through bathroom

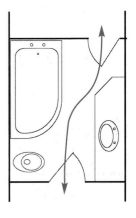

8ft through bathroom

A generous vanity unit with cupboards and a mirror above

Other options

The majority of narrowboats have either enclosed or through bathrooms but these are not the only solutions. If space is particularly tight, you could dispense with the bath or shower tray and use the

circulation space for showering instead. This needs to be considered at an early stage because a watertight compartment has to be formed on the base plate when the shell is built. The fixed floor in the bathroom is replaced by a removable platform with a gap or slots all round to allow the shower water to drip into the compartment below. From here, it is pumped overboard using a dedicated bilge pump. You could install a shower curtain around the circulation space but, if the walls are tiled and all the joints well sealed, you don't really need one.

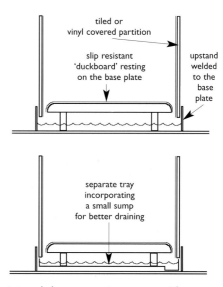

An integral shower requires a watertight compartment on the hull base plate

Using the circulation space for showering forms a 'wet room' (above)

A rare example of an integral shower – note the floor slots for drainage (left)

The advantage of this arrangement is that you can reduce the area of a conventional enclosed bathroom by about a third. Alternatively, it can allow you to have a complete bathroom occupying the space on one side of a central corridor in a smaller boat. The downside is that unless you can incorporate a small sump or you lift the board from time to time and mop up the water that the bilge

pump misses, you are left with $1/2$ in or so of 'grey water' swilling around in that part of the bilge and this can get a bit stale after a while.

Another possibility, which can be useful on boats with a central corridor, is to have separate rooms for the toilet and washbasin on one side of the corridor and the shower or bath on the other. The doors to these two rooms are carefully placed so that they can be opened across the corridor to form a single, larger compartment. When used in this way, this arrangement suffers the same disadvantage as the through bathroom but, if only the toilet or washbasin is needed, the corridor can remain open.

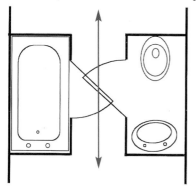

Separate rooms for toilet/ washbasin and for the bath can be linked by doors opening across the central corridor

Equipment

In the seventies and eighties, narrowboat fitters used equipment that was originally designed for caravans. This was slightly smaller than similar items intended for the home so it was easy to fit in but the majority of the equipment for today's narrowboats is bought from a bathroom shop. If you are careful in your choice, you should be able to find items that have a more stylish look without taking up too much space.

The washbasin is usually oval in shape and let into the top of a 'vanity unit' that provides useful storage and sometimes houses the water pump and accumulator or spare cassettes for the toilet. Triangular corner basins can be supported by a unit

A variation on the 'bathroom divided by a corridor' approach

which is custom made to fit. Alternatively, you could opt for an exposed basin set on top of, rather than into, a tiled or marble surface.

Short baths can be simply a 4ft long version of the standard bath or have a raised seat at the end opposite the taps. This is useful as it reduces the amount of water needed to produce a reasonable 'feet-soaking' depth when the bath is used for showering.

A stylish washbasin with taps set in the mirror above

Baths with a raised seat are more versatile

23

Shower trays are very much like the domestic versions but, particularly in an enclosed bathroom, need to be 2ft or 2ft 3in square rather than the normal 2ft 6ins square. There are some very good resin trays which look and feel like porcelain but are much stronger. Glazed shower doors avoid the clammy feel of a nylon shower curtain sticking to you. It may be necessary to order both these items specially – and pay a small premium – in order to get the right size, but it is worth it in the long run.

The toilet is the one item which has to be bought from a specialist supplier. Most holding tank toilets are made from porcelain and, as long as the vogue for white fittings lasts, there should be no difficulty in matching them with the washbasin and bath. Basic toilets are more difficult as they are often made from coloured plastic but they can always be concealed by a timber 'thunderbox' if their appearance concerns you.

There is little condensation in this bathroom where the heated towel rail is connected to the calorifier circuit

Now you see it, now you don't

Small bathrooms can suffer from condensation and, depending on the type of toilet you install, unpleasant smells can linger. The answer here is to expel them through the roof by installing a fan to increase the ventilation. You can buy a solar-powered unit that is specially designed for the job and does not rely on battery power so that it carries on working while you are away.

Another way to reduce condensation – and have constantly warm towels – is to connect the bathroom radiator or heated towel rail to the calorifier circuit rather than the radiator circuit. In this way, whenever you heat the water, the radiator is warmed as well.

⚜

Storage

As with all other parts of the boat, storage space is at a premium in the bathroom and the vanity unit soon becomes full – especially if you decide to locate the pump and accumulator there. One solution is to add a bathroom cabinet on the wall. This could be an off-the-peg model or, preferably, made to match the finishes in the room. Like the wall units in the galley, it should ideally face rearwards so that items inside stay put if you come to a sudden stop.

A bathroom cabinet adds style and some useful storage

Chapter 6

The Bedroom

The bedroom on a narrowboat is different from the other areas in two significant ways. Many of the everyday items used on a boat can be reduced in size slightly so that they fit more easily into the smaller space but, unless you are prepared to sleep in a very cramped position every night, the bed needs to be more or less the same size as the one you sleep in at home.

The second is that, in most cases, the bedroom is only used for about a third of the time you are on the boat and, during that time, you can't really appreciate it because you are sound asleep. Given these circumstances, the logical response might be to design a small bed which expands to full size at night or, better still, can be used for something else during the day.

So much for the theory; in practice, the basic requirement of a large proportion of boat owners is to make the bed in the morning and do nothing to it until they climb back into it at night. A modest pull on the mattress might be acceptable if it means a few extra inches of elbow room but anything that involves the bed disappearing or becoming something that can be used for the other two-thirds of the time gets a definite thumbs down. We start, therefore, with a look at fixed beds.

Fixed beds
Single berths

Single berths can be fitted in fairly easily either side of a central corridor. Being at a low level, the space between them can be slightly narrower than if it were formed by two full height partitions, so the beds can be about 2ft 3in wide. This is less than a standard single bed but is enough for a child or small adult.

If you have a large family of small children, you can accommodate more of them in the same boat length by creating double bunks. The top bunks will be narrower than the lower ones because of the width

Fixed double beds lend themselves to the 'four poster' treatment – even if the middle part of the post is omitted to make it easier to get past

of the gunwale, the inward slope of the cabin side and the fact that it is at elbow height. One way to increase the width of the upper and lower bunks is to move the corridor slightly off centre and have a shallow wardrobe or dressing table opposite.

Slightly off-setting the corridor gives more width for the bunks

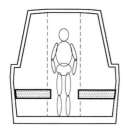

Low-level single beds can project further

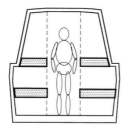

Double bunks are narrower – especially the top one

25

If the top berth is for occasional use, the base and mattress can be designed to be removable. This will make the lower berth feel less claustrophobic when used on its own but you will have to find somewhere to stow the pieces when they are not in place. For very occasional use, you might consider a pipe cot. This consists of a temporary wooden beam or metal tube along the outside edge with a canvas base slung between this and the cabin side.

Double berths

Double berths, being larger in area, are not quite so easy to fit in. The most popular type is the fixed, lengthways bed with a corridor along one side. Naval traditionalists insist that the head of the bed is towards the bow but the only practical benefit of this is where the boat is trimmed bow light and you want to stop the blood rushing to your head.

The maximum width for a fixed, lengthways double is about 4ft, which is only 6in less than a standard double bed but, because it is hard up against the hull side, it feels a lot more restricted.

If you are willing to do some light bed making before turning in, you can increase the bed width by letting down a side flap or sliding the whole bed base out into the corridor. You could have a narrow section of mattress to fill the gap against the hull side but simply pulling a four foot mattress slightly away from the hull side gives the person sleeping on the inside some valuable extra elbow room. This still leaves the other basic drawback of double beds – one partner has to climb over the other to get to the bathroom.

Fixed double bed – the 'inside' partner is rather cramped

Sliding double bed – a few inches of elbow room can make all the difference.

For a really king-size bed, the flap can extend right across the corridor to give you something approaching 6ft 6in square. In this case, the large mattress insert can be hung under the corridor gunwale during the day. Passage through the boat is restricted when the flap is in place and you must make sure that any doors across the corridor are still usable as a means of escape. A further advantage of this arrangement is that, if the bathroom is at the foot end of the bed, either partner can visit there without disturbing the other too much.

Taking the flap idea a stage further, you could decide to sleep across the boat, which means that the bed itself only takes up 4ft 6in to 5ft of boat length instead of the usual 6ft 3in to 6ft 6in. You should ensure that the bed base is no more than about 1ft 3in off the floor or you will not be able to get the pillow under the gunwale at one end and your feet under the other, which limits the effective length of the bed considerably. This arrangement also suffers the disadvantage that, unless you have a bathroom on either side of the bedroom, you are back to one partner climbing over the other.

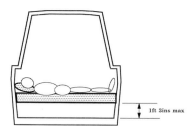

Cross beds – make sure there is enough height for the pillow and your feet

1ft 3ins max

The extra section of mattress can be supported by a hinged flap or, as here, by a telescopic base

Moving beds

Fixed double or single beds are fine if you cruise with the same crew all the time but, if you want to invite a variety of guests, one double or two singles may not always be appropriate. The answer could be to take a leaf from some of the hire operators' books and have movable beds. The bedroom needs to be about 9ft long with doors in the middle at one end and to one side at the other end. A fixed single bed is built in one corner of the bedroom and a matching loose bed is positioned in the diagonally opposite corner. If a double bed is needed, you simply move the beds together and make them up as one.

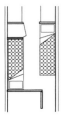

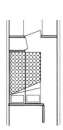

Two beds – one fixed and one movable.
The right hand bed can be moved against the other to make a double

Convertible beds

There are obvious attractions in being able to fall into a ready made bed after a relaxing evening in the saloon or a good meal at the pub but, if dragging eight to ten feet of underused space around with you all day seems a high price to pay for this, you could have a double bed that converts to a dinette during the day.

The amount of space taken up by a double bed and by four people sitting either side of a table are about the same so the two are quite compatible. The centre third of the bed base is a loose board that can be

This convincing looking bed converts to an equally convincing looking dinette by day

supported on the edges of the seat bases either side when in bed mode, or on Desmo legs and sockets when it is a table. The whole assembly is often raised up by 6 or 8 inches so that the diners have a better view out of the window (assuming there is one) and there is more storage space under the seats.

It's a good idea to make the mattress infill as two narrow pieces which then double as backrest cushions in the dinette. If they are slightly oversized, all the pieces press together so that you can hardly feel the joins. You can make the joins even less noticeable if you make up the bed with the seat cushions in the middle and at the head end, and place the two backrests at the foot end.

Assuming you use a duvet, the only really onerous part of making the bed is anchoring the bottom sheet. On our own boat, I have adapted a single duvet cover with bungee cords in each corner that fit over hooks at the four corners of the bed base. It may not be as neat as 'hospital corners' but it does keep it in place and, once I am asleep, I am none the wiser.

Bungee cords keep the bottom sheet firmly in place

Another way to make more use of the space occupied by the bed is to make it pivot upwards into a recess. This approach was used in the back cabins of working boats and we will look at these in more detail later in Chapter eight. Pivoting beds can also be used in modern boats either crossways, in which case it occupies the whole width of the boat, or lengthways, where the corridor is retained.

The whole crossbed is lowered from a recess at night

Free-standing furniture

Free-standing furniture has been popular in the saloon for some time and you can use the same concept in the bedroom. Adapta Designs (01284 750833) has developed a range of free-standing furniture that can be used as single or double beds and then converted to a settee or a table during the daytime if required.

A cosy bedroom under the front deck of a tug

Loose furniture can provide an adaptable solution

Tug decks

Deep draughted tugs with raised front decks often have enough headroom under the deck for a cosy bedroom. To avoid getting trapped in an emergency, you will need to have an escape hatch in the deck above. If this sounds too claustrophobic, the whole bed can be made to slide out at night and back under the deck during the day.

A sliding bed can also be designed to become a settee with its backrest propped against the front bulkhead. As the bed slides into the saloon at night,

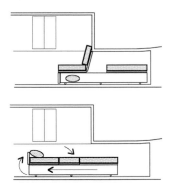

the backrest and cushion drop down to become the middle third of the bed base. Bedding can be stored in the wooden base and, if the door is hinged at the top, it can be fixed in the open position to become the bedhead. Ideally, the front bulkhead should be solid and the side doors positioned a couple of feet back along one or both cabin sides.

Storage

In your desire to save space in the bedroom, try not to be too mean with wardrobe space. Most couples taking a fortnight trip would find anything less than a 3ft wide wardrobe – or two 1ft 6in – rather restricting. Wardrobes positioned against cross bulkheads offer plenty of floor-to-ceiling storage but if they are against the hull side, the depth is more restricted. In this case, assuming that you don't take full length evening

The settee pulls out to become ...

... a bed at night

Wardrobe –a lower rail makes better use of the space

gowns with you when you go off cruising, fix the hanging rail about 4ft from the floor and build in a couple of shelves over it. At this height there will be enough width for clothes to hang at right angles to the rail and still allow room for shoes to be stored below. Mirrors fixed to the fronts of wardrobe doors allow the crew to check that they are properly attired before venturing on deck and also give added space and depth to a small area.

The space under a fixed double or single bed can be very useful for storage provided that you can get to it fairly easily. Single beds are relatively narrow so a drop-down door will give access to the space beneath without the need for arms 5ft long.

Double beds, being wider, require more careful planning. One solution is to make the base that the mattress rests on removable so that you can get at the space from above. The disadvantage is that you have to move the mattress and the bedding before you can do this. A compromise solution is to divide the space beneath the bed lengthwise and have drop-down doors to get to the part adjacent to the corridor. Lift-up lids are then used for the part against the hull side where items you only need once in a while are stored.

A more sophisticated answer is to have drawers that slide on tracks or roll along on fridge runners. The problem is that the drawer could be anything up to 4ft from front to back whereas the corridor into which it opens is only 2ft wide. To overcome this, you could have a 'train' of two or three drawers that are linked so that you pull them out together. When the first one is fully in the corridor, you lift it onto the bed and pull the next one clear.

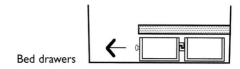

Bed drawers

Chapter 7

The Engine Room

The type of engine room you have is determined by the design of the rear part of the boat. Cruisers and semi-traditional boats – described in Chapter one – have external engine rooms under the rear deck while traditional boats have internal ones, either at the very back, or just forward of a small back cabin.

Regardless of which type you have, the engine needs to be maintained regularly so you need enough space around it to allow you to do this without straining too much. If the job is too difficult or unpleasant, chances are you will be tempted to skimp it or leave it altogether.

External engine rooms

The layout of an external engine room and the size of the access hatch are usually determined by the builder but you should try to ensure that you can get to the engine, and any other pieces of equipment you have specified to go there, without too much difficulty. It's a good idea to have the whole interior painted in a light coloured gloss paint before the equipment is installed. This will resist rusting and make it easier to see what you are doing while you are down there.

The hatch in the rear deck must be designed to allow rainwater to drain away. The opening is often covered by two or three pieces of plywood with a non-slip finish. This means that you can remove one board for routine maintenance tasks, or all of them for more major work. The plywood rests on a series of steel channel sections which act as gutters to direct the rainwater overboard.

This non-traditional engine room allows plenty of working space

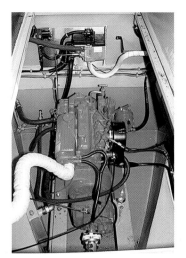

An engine compartment painted in a light colour is much easier to work in. Note the drainage channels around the edge of the opening

Another solution is to weld an upstand around the opening and cover it with a lid like an upturned tray. If this lid is a reasonable size and made of steel, it will be heavy to lift and could drop onto your toes. You could fit gas struts to ease the weight or make it of lighter, corrosion-free aluminium.

Whichever type you have, it is a good idea to make the access panels lockable against theft or vandalism.

Internal engine rooms

Internal engine rooms generally have full head room for at least a part of their area so they can double as wet lockers, drying spaces or stores for folding bikes. Given two or three feet of extra length, they are also an ideal site for washing machines or oil fired boilers. It is a particularly good location for boilers feeding

With a few extra feet, the engine room can serve as an office and utility room

This hatch is almost invisible but a small overlap and a few bolt heads would not have looked out of place

gravity flow central heating systems because most boats are trimmed higher at the bow than the stern so the pipework has a natural rise from the boiler to the radiators further forward. If you allow even more length, the enlarged space can become a study or a utility room – or both.

If you want a really traditional engine room, it should be unlined and painted in red oxide or cream above and dark green below. However, this would suffer from condensation problems at all times of the year so most engine rooms are insulated and lined. They can still be painted in traditional colours but many are scumbled to match the boatman's cabin. Shelves fixed to the forward partition help to keep the room tidy.

The way in which the engine is maintained can have an influence on the layout of the whole boat. Many engines have their service points – dip stick and oil filter – on one side and the pipework for the cooling system on the other side. It therefore makes sense to plan the corridor that goes through the engine room – and through into the rest of the boat – on the side that has the service points. In the majority of engines this is the starboard side, which is why so many boats have the corridor through the rear part of the accommodation on that side.

A point worth considering, particularly if the boat has a vintage engine, is how to get the engine out of the boat for a major overhaul or replacement. One way is to dismantle the engine so that the pieces are small enough, and light enough, to be passed through the side doors. A better way is to have a removable hatch in the roof so that the whole engine can be removed using a hoist.

Some boatbuilders are reluctant to fit hatches,

arguing that it spoils the line of the roof at this critical point where it starts to rise. Others take great pains to make the hatch as unnoticeable as possible by making it flush with the surrounding roof and, in so doing, risk water penetration. It is strange that many boat buyers are happy to spend two or three hundred pounds having false rivets added to the hull yet are so easily persuaded against having a few bolts that actually perform a useful purpose on the roof.

Access

One of the biggest problems of rear engine rooms is how to get past the engine when you want to get to or from the rear deck. If you use an Aquadrive or Python flexible coupling in the drive shaft, it can be run at a sufficient angle to allow the engine to be mounted parallel to the swim on the side opposite the steps.

Installing the engine parallel to the swim improves access

This large hatch and wide steps give exceptionally easy access into the boat

The sound of a vintage engine is part of the canal scene

A wider or longer than normal sliding hatch will lessen the risk of banging your head and also allows a crew member to keep the steerer company without getting in their way.

Vintage engines in traditional engine rooms can also be mounted slightly off-centre by using universal joints on either end of an angled section of the drive shaft.

This idea has been taken a stage further by mounting a smaller modern engine against the hull side in a sound-proof box or under the 'bed'ole' in the boatman's cabin to give near-silent propulsion to an apparently engineless traditional boat.

Universal joints either end of the drive shaft allow the engine to be off centre

Installing a small, modern engine against the hull makes it almost invisible

Soundproofing

Vintage engines proclaim their pedigree with every measured and mellifluous beat, but few of us enjoy the unfettered sound of a modern diesel engine for any length of time.

Sound is carried through the structure of the boat in the form of vibration, and through the air in the form of sound waves, so it has to be tackled in two different ways. Vibration can be controlled by isolating the engine from the rest of the boat and air borne sound can be reduced by cocooning it in a soundproof enclosure. Both of these remedies have an effect on the planning of the boat.

Isolation of the engine from the rest of the boat means flexible mounts, flexible exhaust pipe and a coupling to the propeller shaft which does not allow the vibration of the engine to pass to the hull. Installing flexible mounts without a flexible coupling is fruitless because the vibration will still travel through the remaining rigid connection and, particularly if the distance between the gearbox and the stern tube has been reduced to a minimum, this could shorten the life of the bearing. A flexible coupling may require the length of the engine room to be increased slightly but it is well worth the extra few inches.

Flexible couplings add a few inches but are worth having

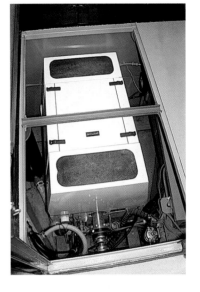

Cocooned engines are quieter but take up more space

Cocooning the engine should be done with special acoustic foam that has a washable surface and a heavy plastic membrane within the thickness – a bit of surplus carpet is just not acceptable any more. The foam is stuck to the underside of the demountable

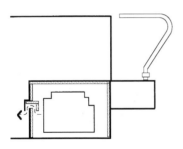

Openings through acoustic foam should avoid direct sound paths.

plywood casing that, in the case of rear engine roomed traditional boats, also forms part of the steps to the rear deck. Where openings occur for controls or combustion air to enter, they should be formed in a way that avoids direct sound paths and lined with acoustic foam.

Some engine manufacturers now produce custom-made, soundproofed casings for their engines which make the job much easier but tend to be rather bulky so more space is required to accommodate them.

If sound reduction is a real priority, you could consider the ultimate solution of mounting the engine midships or even under the front deck and driving the propeller hydraulically.

Chapter 8

The Boatman's Cabin

Boatman's cabins contain a lot of lace, brass – and plates!

When it comes to the merits or otherwise of boatman's cabins, very few boaters sit on the fence. The more traditionally minded extol their virtues as day cabins, 'quiet rooms' or as permanent or occasional bedrooms. But more than that, they are an atmospheric reminder of the days of commercial carrying on the canals. Detractors, on the other hand, argue that they take up space that could otherwise have been used to make the rest of the boat more roomy and that they force anyone of reasonable height to crouch to avoid banging their head on the ceiling – you can't please everyone.

Assuming you are of the first persuasion, you will probably have looked at photographs and actual examples to familiarise yourself with the essential elements. To re-cap, these are a cooking range, a table cupboard, a drop-down cross bed and, on the opposite side, a side bed. These have evolved over years of use to provide the maximum amount of convenient living space in the smallest possible area. Even such things as the position of the stove – on the

port side where the chimney is under the highest part of a tunnel when passing another boat – are the result of a deliberate decision.

The average length of a boatman's cabin in a motor boat is around 8ft, or up to 8ft 6in if it is in a horse boat or butty. The cabin is entered from the rear deck through a pair of doors, centrally placed in the rear bulkhead and from the engine room through a single, centrally placed door. The overall dimension can be reduced to about 7ft 6in or increased to about 9ft 6in but, beyond these sizes, the proportions are altered to such an extent that the cabin no longer looks like the space you are trying to recreate.

Similarly, the headroom should be limited to about 5ft 8in. In a motor boat, this is because the drive shaft from the engine to the propeller runs under the floor, and in a butty, because a lower cabin height is needed so that an unladen boat can get under low bridges. It has also been suggested that the low ceiling height encourages occupants to sit down and, thereby, take up less space.

Using modern technology, it is quite feasible to have full headroom – either by off-setting the engine and running the prop shaft under the cross bed or by driving the propeller hydraulically. If you and your crew are exceptionally tall, these options may be worth considering but think long and hard about it – a boatman's cabin any taller than 5ft 8in just doesn't look 'right'.

Furniture

In earlier chapters, I have dealt with the planning of the spaces in fairly general terms to give you as much freedom as possible to interpret them to your requirements. Traditional boatman's cabins are much more tightly planned and, as we have seen, if they are to work properly and look the part, even a couple of inches can make all the difference.

The most critical dimensions are those along the port side of the cabin where most of the furniture goes. First comes a small but nonetheless important allowance of 2 to 3in for the soap'ole and windlass'ole recesses. The Epping (sometimes known as Classic) stove is about 1ft 10in x 1ft 2in so a dimension of about 2ft 5in is needed if the stove is to be a reasonably safe distance from the surrounding woodwork.

Next is the table cupboard, which should be between 1ft 9in and 1ft 11in wide. It is built out from the cabin side just forward of the stove and its front is angled at about 15° to 20° to the centre line of the boat. This gives the cupboard part of its character

The door drops down to become a table

and funnels people passing through the cabin into the narrow passage in front of the bed cupboard.

A number of factors will determine the width of the final item – the bed cupboard or bed'ole. An original working drawing of a 1935 Yarwoods Northwich shows 3ft – plenty for one but 'cosy' for two. If you plan to use the bed as a double for more than the odd occasion, 4ft should be the minimum, although even this may not be enough if your shell has a low gunwale line. The Yarwoods drawing shows about 1ft 6in from the bed base to the underside of the gunwale so that, even allowing for the mattress and pillow, there is still enough height to make use of the full length of the bed. Most modern shells have a lower gunwale, which means that the effective length of the bed is the distance from cabin side to cabin side – a reduction of about 6 in. One person could still get a comfortable night on a 3ft 0in wide bed by lying slightly diagonally but a tallish couple would need at least 4ft 6in.

Taking the average dimensions and a 4ft wide bed, the boatman's cabin would therefore take up about 8ft 6in of boat length. This is slightly on the high side for a motor boat but would still give the character of the original.

The next question to be decided is the width of the corridor, which, in turn, has an effect on the height of the bed flap. In day mode, this flap is vertical and forms part of the cupboard on the port side with

The soap'ole and windlass'ole are a part of the character

The width of the corridor determines the height of the door of the bedflap

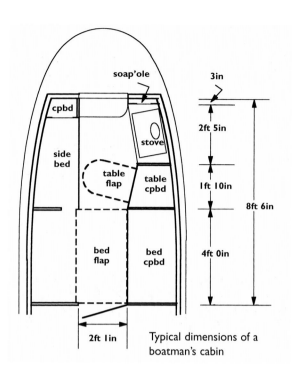

soap'ole

cpbd

side bed

table flap

stove

table cpbd

bed flap

bed cpbd

3in

2ft 5in

1ft 10in

8ft 6in

4ft 0in

2ft 1in

Typical dimensions of a boatman's cabin

doors above and a drawer below. At night, it swings down and rests on a recess in the edge of the bed on the opposite side, forming a continuous platform right across the cabin. It follows, therefore, that the height of the flap needs to be the width of the corridor plus about an inch at top and bottom to rest on the supports either side. On the Yarwoods drawing, this dimension is 2ft 4½in which would result in a 2ft 2½in wide corridor and a correspondingly narrow side bed on most modern boats. A corridor of 2ft 1in and a flap of 2ft 3in is a reasonable compromise.

The height of the side bed depends on whether you go for the authentic boarded top – in which case 1ft 3in to 1ft 5in is the norm – or whether you have permanent cushions – in which case the base height should be around 1ft 2in. With these dimensions and a 5ft 4in headroom, the proportions of the cupboards when all the doors are shut look about right.

Under the bed flap there should be a drawer but a bottom-hinged door looks very similar and makes better use of the space, provided you don't need to get to it too often. Above the bed there is a cupboard that can have a single central door or two doors hinged either on opposite sides or on the same sides, depending on your preference.

The side bed is divided in two by a projection from the cabin side and sometimes a small hinged door, which was originally intended to separate the occupants of the cross bed from children sleeping on the remainder of the bed. In modern use, it is sometimes convenient to use the whole of the side bed as an occasional single berth as, unlike the cross bed, it does not block off the route to the rear doors. If you think you might do this, the projection and door can be omitted as the curtains which divide the cabin into two cover them for most of the time.

A door makes better use of the space below the bed

The two halves of this cabin are divided by a larger than usual partition that also supports a useful shelf over the bed

Alternatives

Although the layout of the boatman's cabin is sacrosanct to the canal purist, there are several variations on the basic theme that may be worth considering if you only want to capture the flavour of the original.

Side Door

The central door into the engine room assumes that the engine is mounted far enough forward to allow you to reach the side corridor without tripping over the gearbox. If you have a very tight engine room, or want to box-in the engine, you might consider a side door. The problem is that there is then no side bed to support the cross bed flap in the horizontal position. Two possible solutions are to increase the height of the bed flap so that it can rest on a ledge on the starboard side or to devise a way of supporting a normal sized flap and another one that drops down from the hull side where they meet.

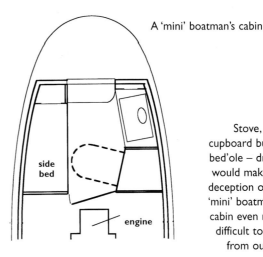

A 'mini' boatman's cabin

Stove, table cupboard but no bed'ole – drapes would make the deception of this 'mini' boatmans's cabin even more difficult to spot from outside

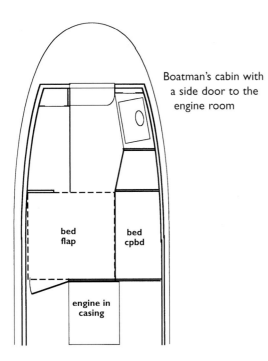

Boatman's cabin with a side door to the engine room

'Mini' Boatman's Cabin

If you want the appearance of a boatman's cabin from outside but cannot really afford the space inside, you could simply limit the cabin to the range and table cupboard with a short side bench opposite. This would make a pleasant boater's day cabin and, with drapes covering the wall to the engine room, would fool all but the most persistent gongoozler. The drawback here is that you would be denying yourself a potentially useful occasional double bed, which you would be hard-pressed to fit into 4ft of cabin length anywhere else on the boat.

Fixed Double Bed

Alternatively, you might decide that the cross bed is not long enough for you or that you don't want the bother of making the bed every night. In this case, you could extend the cabin slightly and have a fixed, lengthways four-poster. Having gone this far, you could then turn the table cupboard into a wardrobe with an arch-topped door. This thought may have dyed-in-the-wool traditionalists spluttering into their real ale but it shows that by using some of the elements and detailing of the original, you can develop a useful and very attractive feature.

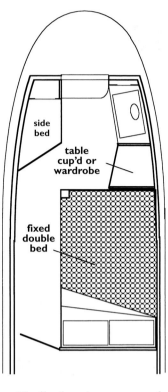

Accommodating a
fixed double bed

side
bed

table
cup'd or
wardrobe

fixed
double
bed

Not strictly
traditional
maybe, but a
very attractive
solution

Finally, there is no reason why a rear cabin should be treated traditionally at all. Its location makes it ideal as a room for younger members of the family to play and sleep without disturbing or being disturbed by the rest of the crew. A rear cabin also allows the engine – which may also be non-traditional – to be located away from the steerer for much quieter cruising.

This back cabin has
many of the elements
of a traditional cabin
but given a more
modern treatment

Chapter 9

Front Decks

Front decks offer a pleasant outdoor sitting area

Most narrowboats have some sort of well deck at the front and this has to be drained to prevent water from entering the cabin. Early ways of tackling this problem involved either allowing the rainwater to run into the permanently wet bilge under the cabin from where it was pumped out occasionally, or piping it back through a dry bilge to the engine room bilge where it could be pumped out.

Neither of these methods is ideal. A permanently wet bilge is likely to produce smells and condensation, which inevitably find their way into the cabin. Drainage pipes can clog with leaves and allow the water on the front deck to rise to possibly dangerous levels.

Self-draining decks

Fortunately there is a simple solution to all these problems – the self-draining front deck. By raising the floor level in the well deck so that it is higher than the normal water line, rainwater that lands on it can be drained overboard via holes or 'scuppers' in the hull side just ahead of the front bulkhead.

Rainwater drains overboard through the scuppers

The only drawback is that since rainwater can drain off the front deck, then canal or river water can enter through the same holes if the boat is unusually heavily laden or if it heels over. This possibility is covered in Section 10 of the Boat Safety Scheme which, although strictly applying only to hire boats and public passenger craft, offers good practice guidance for all boats. It recommends that the holes, and consequently the deck, should be at least 10in above the water line. However, it recognises that this may not always be feasible so, in these cases, boat owners are advised that the sill of any opening from the front deck into the cabin should be at least 6in above the deck.

Self-draining front decks work particularly well for boats of about 1ft 9in draught as the deck level is roughly 1ft 9in above the internal floor level, needing only one internal step. The gunwale is about 1ft 6in above the deck so fixed seats can be incorporated on either side for outdoor lounging or to act as a step when getting on and off the boat.

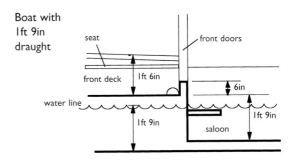
Boat with 1ft 9in draught

They do not work quite so well on boats with 2ft to 2ft 3in draught. These require the front deck to be about 2ft 3in above internal floor level, which means a higher step, or even a small set of steps, is needed to get to the deck and the reduced deck-to-gunwale height usually rules out any side seats.

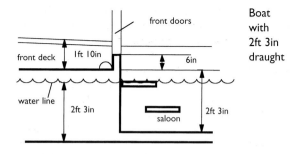

Boat with 2ft 3in draught

Whether or not you have fixed seats is a matter of personal choice. A large, open deck can accommodate a couple of director chairs and a small table that can be removed when they are not needed, leaving plenty of space for other things. On the other hand, fixed side or cross seats can be useful and are always there whenever you feel the need for a rest.

The space under these fixed seats inevitably gets used for storing deck gear, dog bowls and the like and these can look very untidy when viewed from the saloon. One answer is to fill in the front and turn the seat into a locker, but this needs to be done with caution. Water, either from rain or condensation, is almost bound to collect in the base of the locker and, in time, start to rust the inside. Once this gets a hold it is not easy to cure so make sure that the locker is well drained and ventilated and resolve to paint the inside regularly.

Tug decks

You could, of course, dispense with the well altogether and have the deck at, or just below, the level of the gunwales. This gives an appearance similar to the working tugs that had their holds covered by stout boards so the style has become

known as a tug deck. In order to give the right proportions, the deck needs to be at least 6ft long and preferably more. The space underneath it can be used as a large storage locker or, as we saw in Chapter six, used as a bedroom.

Tug decks offer a large platform on which you can stand a table and chairs for alfresco meals. They are also less likely to allow water into the cabin in 'choppy' conditions on rivers. On the downside, you have to be especially careful not to trip and topple over the edge and you need a taller flight of steps, and possibly a sliding hatch over the front doors, to enable you to get into the cabin more easily.

Lowered decks

Self-draining and tug decks may eliminate the need to pump out the bilge from time to time but there is a solution that enables you to lower the deck without having a wet bilge under the cabin. This entails creating a watertight upstand under the front bulkhead to contain any rain that lands on the front deck. You still have to pump it out occasionally, or install a reliable automatic bilge pump, but you can then use the front deck more as an extension of the saloon.

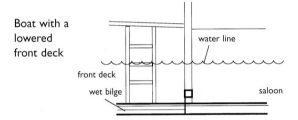

Boat with a lowered front deck

You could take the idea a stage further by extending the roof of the cabin over the front deck and supporting it on inspection launch style columns or on a cratch board. The open sides can then be fitted with removable transparent screens to keep out the weather. This creates a sort of conservatory where you can eat or just admire the scenery without being totally exposed to the elements. The enclosure has a further benefit in considerably reducing the amount of rain that falls on the deck, so the bilge pump should only be needed in emergencies.

Tug decks provide an ideal platform for a table and chairs

This front deck has full headroom and protection from the weather

The cratch board or, more correctly, 'deck board' of a working boat is the triangular board over the front deck beam that supports the top plank which, in turn, support the cloths over the hold. On a modern boat, the cratch board can be as simple as a piece of stout plywood or as complicated as your imagination, and you or your builder's wood-working skills, can make it.

The main problem with fixed cratches is that they make access to the front deck or the gas locker rather difficult. A popular way round this is to have a central post supporting the beam and hinged triangular wings, one on either side. The wings can be swung back when access is required and, if you use lift-off hinges, removed completely.

The wings swing back to give access to the gas locker

One drawback to this arrangement is that while it is much easier to move between the saloon and the front deck, getting from the front deck to the bank involves a rise of about 3ft. Nimble boaters will manage this with one intermediate step but less agile ones, or large, clumsy dogs, may need a safe flight of steps – ideally on both sides.

Cratches

Of all the parts of a working narrowboat that have been copied or adapted on modern cruising boats, the cratch is probably the most useful. Whether the deck is self draining or lowered, it provides a reasonably dry storage space for things you don't want in the cabin, shelter from wind and rain while cruising and a 'porch' in which to dry the dog and shed muddy boots before setting foot in the cabin.

Another variation is to incorporate a drop-down table into the cratch. How successful this is will depend on the relative heights of the well deck and surrounding gunwale but, for most boats, it works well. The triangular table is hinged at the bottom and, usually, supported by a hinged leg at the back. The fixed part of the cratch board can be solid or, for a better view from the table, glazed. If you go for this option, the table top can be decorated with traditional roses or triangles so that they show through the glass when raised, but you will need to varnish it well to prevent cups

The cratch board and top plank with the covers removed

The table can drop down when needed

and plates from wearing them away. Whichever type you chose, it is also a good idea to make the whole assembly easily removable for maintenance.

When it comes to choosing a cover for the front deck, you could have a shortened version of the traditional cloths, complete with coiled strings, but most owners opt for a more modern design. These are usually made from a fabric-backed vinyl or PVC-coated polyester, although natural and synthetic fabrics are gaining ground. Transparent panels can be let into the sides for more light but these tend to be the first part to fail.

The covers are held in place by a combination of turnbuckles, lift-off studs and bungee rubber loops. One vertical zip towards the back of the side panel makes it easier to open up from inside. Adding a second zip somewhere near the middle allows you to leave the front half down and the rear half rolled up for sheltered cruising in less than perfect weather.

Two zips are more versatile

Fore decks

At the very front of the boat is a small triangular locker, which is generally used to house the gas bottles. Holes to the outside, similar to the deck scuppers, must be provided at the lowest level so that any gas leaks will drain directly overboard and not collect in the locker. This arrangement works well on boats with a draught of around 1ft 9in because the floor of the locker can be well above water level and still leave enough headroom for a 13kg gas bottle. If any water from a turbulent lock does find its way in, it will soon drain out leaving the locker to dry.

Boats with a greater draught are more of a problem because the floor of the locker needs to be much nearer to the water level and, in some cases, may be below it. Holes for gas drainage must still be provided, so the locker may be permanently wet. In this case, it must be maintained regularly to ensure that the inside does not start to rust and eventually allow water to enter the boat.

To avoid this situation arising, several solutions have been tried. Perhaps the simplest is to ballast the boat so that the bow is not as deep in the water as the stern. This may be effective but it gives the boat a rather nose-up appearance, which I find less appealing than a more level trim. Another is to use smaller gas bottles so that the locker does not need to be so tall, but these need changing more frequently. Some owners specify a raised locker lid or even a mini fore cabin to increase the headroom over the bottles. Whether you go for this option depends largely on whether you like the resulting appearance.

This raised gas locker resembles a small fore cabin

Holes for gas drainage must be provided at the lowest level of the gas locker – even if this is below the waterline

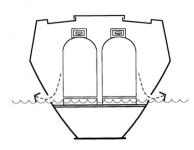

Chapter 10

The Shell and Services

The Shell

Many of the planning possibilities we have looked at can be accommodated without having any effect on the shell but there are some that do. There are also some standard features of a shell that, with a little thought, could be modified to make your boating easier and more enjoyable.

Width of the gunwale

In a normal day's cruising on a narrowboat, you and your crew will need to get quickly from the front to the back of the boat many times. Going through the cabin is the safest way but a certain amount of the towpath is bound to find its way in on your boots and this may not improve your popularity rating, especially if you have light carpets. It may also be that you have opted for a through bathroom and someone has decided to use it.

The simple alternative is to use the side decks or gunwales but, if you do, they should be a minimum of 4in, and better still, 5in wide. Whichever width you choose, they will be more effective if the outer edge is welded to a square profile and not folded to a rounded one as most builders do.

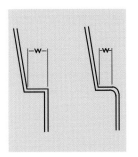

Square profile gunwales give more effective width

Wider gunwales mean that the space between the cabin sides is decreased but this could be partly overcome by having the hull sides vertical from top to bottom with no fold below the top guard.

Height of the gunwale

Most modern narrowboats have a gunwale line that is lower than on traditional working boats. This means that the narrower part of the interior – between the cabin sides – is increased while the wider part – between the hull sides – is decreased, making the overall interior width feel tighter. As noted in chapters six and eight, it also makes it difficult to have a full length cross bed.

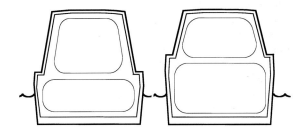

Higher gunwales give more internal space

Raising the gunwale line is not without its problems as the level of the window sill is also raised, making it more difficult to see out of the boat when sitting inside. Some builders have tried to overcome this by lowering the gunwale line where the saloon windows occur and raising it on either side. This solution is a trap for the unwary when walking the gunwales – no matter how wide they are – and has never found favour with private boaters.

Lowered gunwales have never found favour with private boaters

Weed hatch

Modern narrowboats have what is optimistically termed a 'weed hatch' over the propeller, although this is normally used for removing man-made items, which may involve a hacksaw or bolt croppers. The upstand around the opening is a screwed-down lid that has to be removed before you can get to work. If the boat has a cruiser or semi-traditional stern, access to the weed hatch is quite easy once the deck boards are raised.

Traditional boats are more difficult, requiring the owner to crawl under the rear deck and sometimes past the engine as well. Painting this area in a light

This type of weedhatch needs a long arm

colour and installing a light makes the job easier. To avoid this problem altogether, some builders extend the weed hatch upstand to an opening in the rear deck covered by a hatch. This allows access from outside but, on a deep draughted boat, the distance between the surface of the rear deck and the propeller can be as much as 3ft. It is not too difficult to remove polythene bags with a sharpened boathook but any job requiring you to get a hand down to the propeller could mean stripping off or being towed to a dry dock.

A better solution is to provide a hinged lid in the rear deck that lifts to reveal a conventional weed hatch below. For security,

The hatch in the deck lifts to reveal a conventional weed hatch below

the lid can be hinged at the back and held down by the rear cabin doors when the boat is left.

Incidentally, the upstand around the hatch should be of at least the same thickness as the hull sides or it may rust through in time and allow water into the boat.

Height of the tiller

Whether you choose a traditional or cruiser shell, make sure that the tiller is at a height that you find comfortable. Traditional boats with tall cabin sides sometimes have very high tillers, which mean that your arm is permanently raised when steering. Some cruisers go to the other extreme of having a very low tiller that makes it impossible to stand in a comfortable position and see over the cabin. Somewhere round about waist level is usually the most comfortable.

A tiller at waist height is less likely to strain your arm or your back

Wheelhouse

Cruising a narrowboat in wet weather means donning the waterproofs or raising the umbrella, which should keep you reasonably dry. However, some owners incorporate a wheelhouse or helm shelter which, to my eye, look rather out of place on a narrowboat.

Wheelhouses have a further drawback in that, if they are to offer standing headroom inside, they generally have to be removed to get under low canal bridges. And if it happens to be raining at the time, you are back to the waterproofs or an umbrella. You also need to ensure that any water that lands on the floor of the wheelhouse drains overboard and not into the cabin or engine compartment.

One builder has proved that it is possible for a narrowboat to have a fixed wheelhouse by keeping the external height to a minimum, sloping the sides to follow the curve of bridges or tunnels and

Imagine getting this under a low canal bridge!

Fixed weights are dealt with quite simply as they can either be counterbalanced by putting more ballast on the opposite side or they can be made to cancel one another out. If the battery bank is on the starboard side at the rear of the plan, try to arrange it so that the stove is on the port side near the front.

Variable weights require more thought. The water tank is usually at the front of the boat and the diesel tank is usually at the rear but the length of most boats, and the fact that the tanks are generally topped up regularly, mean that the effect these have on the longitudinal trim is fairly limited. Toilet holding tanks can be located virtually anywhere on the boat and can have a marked effect on the sideways trim of the boat. The best way to avoid this is to position them on the centre line of the plan.

providing ballast tanks that lower the whole boat for negotiating exceptionally low bridges.

Roof rack

If you plan to use your boat for extended cruising, you will find you need more storage space and it may be inevitable that items like bikes or logs are kept on the roof. This can damage the roof finish and, if rainwater collects for any length of time, the whole paint system will suffer and the steel roof could start to rust. These problems can be avoided by providing a removable roof rack so that the items are raised above the roof and the surface underneath can be cleaned and maintained easily.

The fixed weight calorifier on the left can be counter balanced. The more variable holding tank is better placed on the centre line

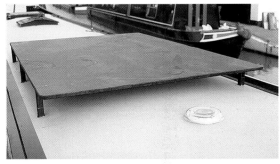
A separate roof rack is better for storage

Weight distribution

I have already mentioned the effect that lop-sided plans have on ballasting but there are certain heavy objects, common to all boats, which need to be considered as well. These can be divided into two types: there are those like the battery bank and a solid fuel stove which have a fixed weight, and those like the water and holding tanks in which the weight varies depending on how full they are.

The eye of the beholder

Finally, spare a thought for the proportions of the shell. As you refine the internal layout of the boat, you will probably find that some parts take up more room than you originally anticipated. You could always order a longer shell but if it is already the maximum size to fit into your mooring or to cruise the northern canals, chances are that you will be tempted to reduce the lengths of the front and rear decks.

This seemingly easy solution has two drawbacks. First, the external areas of the boat, like the internal ones, need to be a certain size in order to work properly. A rear deck that is too small may be less safe, a short front deck may not allow enough space for all the crew to enjoy the open air and an undersized fore deck may make it more difficult to change the gas bottles.

A longer boat needs longer decks to balance it

Second, boats with over-large cabins look ungainly, which could make them more difficult to sell. If your boat is less than 50ft long, there is also a chance that you may want to extend it in the future. Decks that are only just long enough at the original length look far too small with another 8ft or 10ft of cabin in between them, so try to think ahead and be generous.

As a rough rule of thumb, traditional boats over 55ft should have a rear deck of 3ft 6in, a front deck of not less than 4ft 6in and a fore deck of 5ft. You might reduce these slightly on a shorter boat provided you are certain that you, or a future buyer, will not want to have it lengthened.

Services
When making the considerable investment that a new narrowboat represents, you will naturally want to make sure that the plan reflects your needs and preferences. Provided these are not compromised too much, it is worth considering whether one or two slight adjustments might improve the way the services operate.

Most of the equipment on the boat will require a pipe or a cable leading to or from it to enable it to work. The pipes supplying water to the basins or gas to the cooker and boiler are generally arranged like a tree with a 'trunk' taking it most of the way and 'branches' coming off it to supply the individual fittings. This is much easier to achieve if all the fittings are on one side of the boat rather than being dotted about over the plan.

If this is not possible, you may have to run a 'trunk' down each side of the boat but this means that the number of joints and, therefore, the chances of a leak, are increased. This is inconvenient where water pipes are concerned, but is a lot more serious in the case of gas.

In your quest to get the most accommodation into the confines of your shell, you may also be sorely tempted to tuck items like the calorifier, and even the engine, away in tight corners to make room for other, more interesting things. This is understandable but you should bear in mind that no matter how good the equipment you choose, and how well you or your builder install it, at some stage you will need to get to it and the cables or pipework that serve it for maintenance, repairs or modifications.

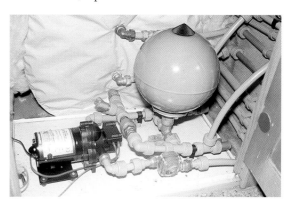

This pump, filter and accumulator can be reached easily at the bottom of the vanity unit

It has been suggested that the best way to achieve this is to complete all the woodwork first and then install the equipment, pipes and cables. This is, perhaps, a bit drastic but you should always allow for reasonable access in the form of access panels or demountable furniture and not conceal pipes and cables permanently behind expensive woodwork. If you do, there is a well-known law that decrees that these are the parts you will need to get at.

Chapter 11

Turning it into Reality

If you have worked your way through the preceding chapters, you probably have a few ideas starting to form in your mind but how do you turn these into a plan that you can give to your builder?

Tricks of the trade

The skill of the designer is one that takes students of engineering or interior design many years to acquire but here are a few tips to help you get started

- When designing anything – from the overall layout to the most detailed piece of furniture – always start with the parts you cannot alter and work towards the parts that you can. First, position the immovable things like the engine, water tank and door positions and then think about the double bed or bathroom whose size is fixed but whose location is more flexible. Lastly, work on the larger, open plan areas like the saloon where a few inches one way or the other are not so critical.
- Try to produce as many different layouts as you can rather than homing in too soon on one that more or less works. As my father, also an architect, used to say, when all the possible solutions are laid out in front of you, you don't have to be a genius to pick the best one.
- Narrowboats are, by their very nature, long and narrow so they do not fit easily onto an oblong sheet of paper. If you do not have a very large drawing board, you might be tempted to work on half the plan at a time but this will not give you the overall picture. It is best to do your preliminary sketches of the whole boat at a smaller scale and then, when you are reasonably happy with that, draw it out, in two or three parts if necessary, to a larger scale. A scale of ¼in:1ft or

You may have something like this in your mind's eye but how do you turn it into reality?

1:50 is about right for the overall plan while the detailed plan should be at ½in:1ft or 1in:1ft (roughly 1:20 or 1:10).

- Finally, the essential elements of a good design were defined in Roman times as 'firmness, commodity and delight' and this is still true today. In your keenness to ensure that the partitions do not fall over and the corridor is wide enough, try not to lose sight of the 'delight factor' which will give you a buzz every time you step on board.

Blueprint for success

One way to start would be to pin a fresh piece of paper to a drawing board, take a sharp pencil and work your way from the front to the back, drawing your layout as you go. Unfortunately, unless you are a second Leonado da Vinci, the chances of getting to much beyond the front doors without wanting to change something are pretty slim.

A more flexible method is to simply draw the outline of the boat and some of the fixed features like the front and rear decks and the engine. It's a good idea to draw a grid within the outline so that you have some idea of scale. If you divide the width of the boat by three and then divide the length by about the same dimension, you arrive at a grid of a little over 2ft by 2ft. This is very useful because most items in the boat will fit neatly into one or more squares of this size. A double bed is three by two squares while a single bed is three by one square. A conventional enclosed bathroom can be fitted into three by two squares and the corridor linking all the spaces is one square wide. This grid is not totally precise but it is near enough and has sufficient in-built margins for error to allow for the thickness of partitions to be added later.

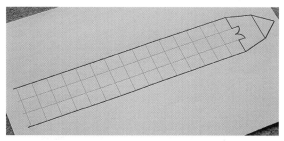

An outline sketch with 2ft grid

Once you have drawn your outline, you can lay a piece of tracing paper over it and sketch away with a soft pencil or felt tip pen, refining your design as you go. If you need to change part of the plan, you can either rub it out or lay another piece of tracing paper over the first and work on that.

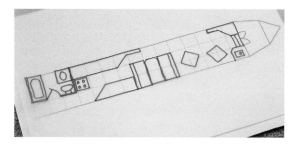

Tracing paper allows you to refine your layout

Alternatively, you could draw all the pieces of furniture and equipment you plan to include on a

separate piece of thin card, cut them out and then move them over the outline drawing until you find the layout that is right for you. The diagram at the end of this chapter gives the sizes of some of the items found on a narrowboat. If you have definitely decided that you are going to have a particular feature like a conventional enclosed bathroom, it is easier to cut out one piece for the whole room rather than several small ones. It also helps if you write or draw on each piece of card to remind you what it represents.

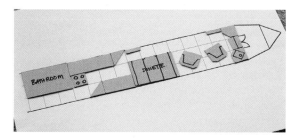

Pieces of card can also be used to help you plan

Into the electronic age

I planned our present boat using the tracing paper method but, if I ever built another, I would use a computer. Over the years, I have been asked many times if there is a program to assist you to plan a narrowboat and the answer is that it depends what you are looking for. If you want a tailor-made program with the hull shape and all the pieces of equipment beautifully drawn out ready for you to assemble into your dream boat, the answer is that I do not know of one. The good news, however, is that you don't really need that. If your computer has a basic drawing program on it – and most of them have – you can use it in a similar way to the methods I have already described.

Start by drawing an outline of the boat with a grid

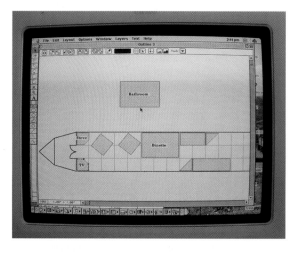

Manual or electronic, the principles are the same.

superimposed and, around the edge, some of the pieces of furniture and equipment you intend to use. You can then add, move and erase these pieces on the plan but, instead of doing it with a pencil or pieces of card, you do it electronically. Of course it looks much better if the bow has a graceful curve on it and the gas hob has all the burners shown but these are not essential. As long as you know which is the front and which is the back, and the overall dimensions of the equipment are reasonably accurate, a few simple straight lines, squares and circles are all that is needed at this stage.

With a couple of hours of practice, you will find that you can move things around far more easily on screen than you can on paper. Another advantage is that the scale of the drawing is not so important because you can zoom in and out for a detailed or an overall view.

All the drawings in this book were done using a computer aided design (CAD) program that is only slightly more sophisticated than the drawing packages that come with most computers. There are several good CAD programs on the market now and some, like Turbocad, allow you to work on different layers, rather like the tracing paper method. If you have one of these, you can draw the outline and grid on one layer of the drawing and then work out the layout on a different layer. This may prevent you erasing more than you intended when you need to alter something.

How far should you go?

If you are having the boat built by a professional builder, it is probably better not to do much more than this basic layout drawing. Most builders have their own ways of planning the boat in detail and will probably prefer you to go along with it. Your drawing will be enough to show the builder the way you are thinking and enable you to come to an agreement about the final plan. The builder may even be able to suggest ways to improve your plan that had never occurred to you.

If, on the other hand, you are planning to fit out the boat yourself, you will need to produce a much more detailed layout so that you can tell the shell builder exactly where the doors, windows and service outlets should be positioned. The layout will also show you whether your ideas will work in practice or whether you have been too optimistic. Remember, it is much easier and cheaper to rectify your mistakes if you discover them on paper – or on the computer screen – than if they come to light after the shell has arrived and you are half way through the fit out.

To help you with the more detailed planning, here are the sizes of a few pieces of equipment found on most narrowboats.

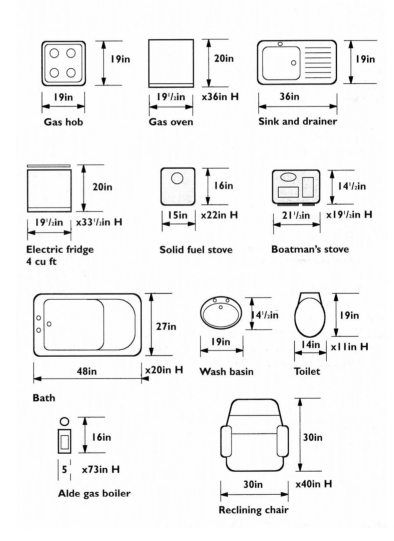

To help you to plan your boat these are the typical sizes of the equipment you are likely to want to incorporate in your layout.

Chapter 12

Putting on the Style

All of the furniture and fittings I have described so far in this book would work perfectly well if they were made from plain sheets of plywood screwed together at the corners and given a coat or two of gloss varnish. However, a glance at the photographs accompanying the descriptions reveals that the designers of the boats have given them character and atmosphere by opting for a particular style of fitting out.

The whole concept of style is sometimes scorned by boaters of the 'old school' who consider that a narrowboat is a purely functional item and see this as a step in the direction of TV makeover shows. I can sympathise with this to a point but I feel that, as well as needing to be able to travel around the canal system efficiently and safely, a modern narrowboat has many of the attributes of a house. It is, therefore, only natural that its owners want an interior in which they feel comfortable and which expresses their personality. Moreover, this desire can be traced back to the earliest days of canal transport.

Early days

The first narrowboats had a tiny cabin with minimal comforts where the crew could shelter before returning to their house 'on the bank' at the end of the trip. The coming of the railways forced down wages to such an extent that many boatmen had to give up their houses and move their families onto the boats. They brought some of their smaller possessions and ornaments with them and set about making the insides of the cabins as 'homely' as possible.

The style they adopted needed to be as cheap and effective as possible. They could not afford the elaborately panelled hardwood doors which were popular with the middle and upper classes so they imitated these with mouldings tacked around the edges of square framing. The whole cabin was then comb grained using a

Opposite: Scumbled woodwork, castle scenes, brass fittings and ribbon plates give an inviting look to this reproduction of a boatman's cabin.

yellow undercoat and 'scumble' to resemble hardwoods and give a warmer, more luxurious appearance. Paintings were neither affordable nor practical so they developed the familiar castle scenes. These are very similar in style to the landscapes painted on the back of glass which were also popular in the Victorian period. The scenes were painted onto door panels so that the moulding around them

Many of the elements of a boatman's cabin can be seen in this interior of a showman's caravan. The ceiling even has floral painting that is very similar to the garlands of roses on the door panels of a narrowboat except that, in this case, they are incorporated into a more classical style of decoration.

doubled as a picture frame. Add a few ribbon plates, some lace edging and a brass oil lamp and you have an interior that must have been very welcoming after a long, wet day.

Although not strictly narrowboats, inspection launches were canal craft in which not only the style of fitting out was determined by their purpose but also outward appearance. In the days when canals were owned by separate companies, it was customary for the directors to make periodic inspections of their assets. Because the dignity of the board members had to be maintained, a simple conversion of a working boat was out of the question. These boats were therefore modelled on more socially acceptable Thames launches. Inside, the main cabin was a cross between a Victorian boardroom and a gentleman's club with real hardwood panelling and carved scrolls, etched glass windows and richly upholstered seating. This no doubt served to insulate the directors from the harsh realities of canal life but how much they actually learned from their trip is questionable.

Another group of 'liveaboard' workers of this period were the showmen who travelled around the country with their steam engines and fairground attractions. They also wanted to take all the home comforts with them and, although they could afford a better standard of finish, their caravans contained many of the elements of a boatman's cabin including a coal fired range, horse brasses, bracket oil lamp and wall plates.

The first leisure boats

Apart from a few working boats converted for cruising or residential use in the forties and fifties,

the first boats designed for leisure appeared in the 1960s. Many of these were built for hire and their standard of the fit out reflected the pioneering nature of canal cruising in those days.

Looking back at the earliest editions of *Waterways World*, it is evident that there were two main 'schools' of boat fitting. First, there was the melamine sheet with mahogany trim approach, probably borrowed from river cruisers of the time. The white or cream coloured sheet made the cabin seem lighter and airier as well as being easy to clean and very hard wearing. The varnished hardwood trim was equally durable and provided an attractive contrast.

The second style stemmed from one of the methods of building the superstructure. Hardwood frames that followed the line of the cabin sides and roof were fixed at intervals along the steel hull, spanning from one gunwale to the other. These frames were then clad in thick tongued and grooved boarding which became both the structure and the internal lining material. Finally, the outer surface of the boarding was covered with sheets of Masonite – an oil tempered hardboard – to keep the weather out.

At about this time, knotty pine boarding was a popular cladding material for 'feature walls' in homes so, since the cabin sides and roof were already boarded, it seemed natural to use this material for the hull lining, partitions and fixed furniture as well. This style became so well established that, when all-steel shells became the norm, thinner boarding was used to line the cabin sides and roof.

T&G boarding is easy to fit around obstructions like pipes and windows and its natural insulating properties must have been appreciated at a time when thermal insulation was not as good as it is

White melamine with dark hardwood trim gave a hard wearing interior.

Knotty pine T&G boarding as far as the eye can see.

nowadays. However, it suffered the drawbacks of darkening with age, making the cabin increasingly dingy. More importantly, it created parallel lines along the interior which emphasised its already long and narrow proportions. At best, the general effect was of a sauna but most resembled the inside of a varnished shed.

By the nineteen eighties, the popularity of knotty pine was in decline and there were many boatbuilders coming into the business bringing fresh ideas with them. Their response was to line the cabin and construct the furniture using hardwood veneer faced plywood and matching solid cappings. Customers wanted lighter interiors so oak and ash were the most commonly used materials. The result may sound fairly bland but it has the advantage that it can be personalised easily by the use of curtains, upholstery and pictures.

Some established builders followed this trend while other made subtle changes to their old methods. White melamine on cabin sides and furniture became light wood grain melamine, giving

Veneered plywood and solid cappings relieved by soft furnishings.

Above: A 21st century interior with ash fitted furniture and, in this case, ash T&G lining. The light coloured hardwood combined with blue soft furnishings and an absence of mouldings gives a cool, unfussy look which is very popular today.

Left: Also in ash but with lots of mouldings and interesting joinery details, this interior shows that modern materials can be combined with traditional construction to great effect.

an equally hard wearing but less clinical look. The ceiling generally remained white to reflect as much light as possible. Pine T&G boarding gave way to parana pine and later oak or ash. This had a more upmarket appearance and was less prone to darkening.

In some cases, T&G cabin sides were teamed with veneer faced ply ceilings or vice versa in order to reduce the tunnel effect. Other builders tried fixing the cabin side boarding diagonally rather than along the length of the cabin although this can produce other strange optical effects. There was also the hybrid approach of using

Below: With its mahogany washstand, deep red wallpaper and period light fittings, this Victorian style bathroom is perfectly in tune with the traditional lines of the boat that contains it.

Below right: This interior shows how tongued and grooved oak boarding combined with a contrasting mahogany trim is much more interesting and luxurious than the pine boarded cabins from which it evolved. The glass fronted display cabinets have something of the character of the showman's caravan earlier in this chapter.

Above: If you compare this picture with the illustration on page 52, you can see how far hire boats have come in the last twenty years. In essence, it follows the melamine and hardwood trim tradition but the cabin sides are now covered in textured vinyl and the hardwood is a warm mid brown. Set off by carefully chosen curtains, cushions and upholstery, it produces a very attractive interior.

Left: Narrowboats are sometimes referred to as 'floating cottages' but few deserve the title more than this one. The plywood lining is painted white to suggest plaster and there are stained timber 'beams' in the ceiling giving a half timbered look. The stove is along the side of the saloon and the stove pipe is concealed by a 'chimney breast' and a beaten copper canopy. Chintz curtains and upholstery, framed pictures and small items of furniture all add to the very domestic feel of this interior.

Bottom left: Gloss painted mahogany is normally considered too dark for narrowboats – especially those with portholes – and is more often associated with upmarket river cruisers. However, as this example shows, if used sensibly and teamed with rich velvet upholstery and thick pile carpets, it can give a very sumptuous atmosphere.

Below : A very individually styled saloon with joinery and lining in various gloss varnished hardwoods and a light coloured ceiling. What makes this interior particularly interesting is the use of parts salvaged from pieces of antique furniture, like the bow topped display cabinet.

dark hardwood trim with lighter T&G boarding to provide some contrast.

The leisure revolution

The nineteen nineties saw an enormous increase in the demand for narrowboats as many couples took early retirement and started extended cruising or even living aboard. Like the boating families of the nineteenth century, they wanted a floating home from home and the boatbuilding industry responded to the challenge. Some builders called on in-house skills while others employed professional interior designers but, whichever it was, the general standard of design and fit out improved noticeably during this period.

Another type of customer to emerge around this time was the 'trophy boat' buyer who wanted a boat that nobody else had. It might be one with a novel form of propulsion or enough generating power to run a small village but, more often than not, it was one with an exotic style of fitting out. Since narrowboats are based on working boats from the nineteenth century, the obvious style to adopt for anyone wanting to go beyond the accepted norm is Victorian but, as the following examples show, with a little thought and imagination, virtually anything is possible.

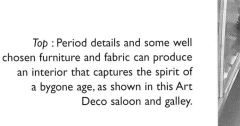

Top : Period details and some well chosen furniture and fabric can produce an interior that captures the spirit of a bygone age, as shown in this Art Deco saloon and galley.

Inspired by modern loft apartments, this interior uses light coloured hardwoods and chrome rather than brass fittings to create a minimalist look.

Left: Apart from the occasional arch, most of the lines in a narrowboat interior are straight but, as this example shows, curves can help to distract your eye from the long and narrow proportions. The route through the galley sways gently from side to side before arriving at the elliptical dinette seating. The two areas are separated by a curved room divider which continues the theme in the vertical plane.

Below: Every now and again, someone decides that narrowboat design needs to be 'revolutionised' and employs an interior designer or architect, often with no experience of boating, to do the deed. The result has all the ambiance of a nineteen sixties British Rail waiting room, and the boat is quietly sold off a few months after the launch for a fraction of what it cost to build.

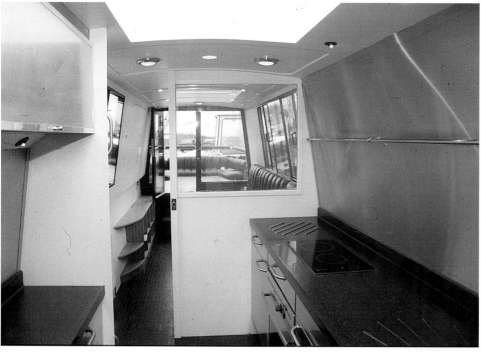

Above and left: The owners of this boat wanted an Art Deco style interior but was concerned that this might make it difficult to sell when the time came. They therefore added a few well chosen details to an otherwise conventional fit out.

Details

Above : This boat is fitted out entirely in 'cat's paw' oak. The joinery is rich in detail as this part of the cabin and roof lining show. Note that the framing looks more convincing because the vertical members in the cabin sides line through with the cross members in the roof.

Right: Using T&G boarding vertically below the gunwale not only avoids the tunnel effect but gives the character of a wainscot.

Below: These details give a more classical appearance to the interior. The Adam style fireplace has two 45° bends so that it fits into a corner around the stove which is also set at 45°. The acorn finials are on the four corners of the bed/dinette and are appropriate in a boat that is fitted out in oak. The corbel and fluted column carry the theme through to other pieces of fitted furniture throughout the boat.

Above: This interior is lined out in a fairly conventional way with framing and panels except that, instead of using veneered ply or T&G boarding for the panels, they are ordinary plywood covered with wallpaper. Many people imagine that wallpaper will be easily damaged or start to peel off in damp conditions but, if a suitable durable paper is chosen and it is well pasted at the edges, it survives as well as most other finishes. The advantages are that, if it is damaged, it can be repaired or replaced easily and, if you get tired of the colour or pattern, you can change the whole character of the boat in a couple of days.

Finishes

Left: Natural timber can be stained before it is varnished to give added colour and, if the stain is thinned, the graining on the wood will show through. This galley is entirely in shades of blue but the other spaces in the boat are all treated quite differently so that each has its own individual character.

Above: Scumble is not the only 'false finish' that can be used. Various marbling techniques have been combined here to create an interior where nothing is quite what it seems.

Above : The outside of this boat is in the original BW blue and yellow livery so the owner decided to carry the theme through to the bedroom. The main areas are primrose yellow while the details – including the fluting on the columns – are picked out in blue.

Right: A variety of finishes have been used in this interior to give a bright, colourful atmosphere. The cabin sides and ceiling are painted, the framing is natural timber and the lower woodwork has a dark red stain. The white paintwork and timber framing are continued throughout the rest of the boat but the accent colour is different in each space.

Part 2

The second part of this book contains reviews of narrowboats of all kinds from 30ft to 70ft. Some parts of the boats will be familiar because they have been used to illustrate points in the earlier chapters while others are seen for the first time.

The boats have been chosen from the many I have reviewed because they are representative of a type of layout or because they show what can be done with a little thought and ingenuity. In some cases, two boats are reviewed together to demonstrate how boats that, in some ways, are very similar can be made to look and perform quite differently by altering the layout.

Fabis

A 30ft traditional-style narrowboat with a number of planning options

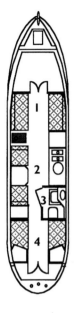

1 Saloon   4ft 0in
2 Galley/
  dinette   6ft 3in
3 Bathroom   3ft 3in
4 Rear cabin   4ft 9in

Fabis is one of a class of 30ft production boats built by Davison Brothers of Sawley Bridge and known, appropriately, as a Short Boat. Designed in the 1970s the boats drew both from glass fibre cruiser and narrowboat technology. In spite of its diminutive length, *Fabis* has a rear deck which, at 3ft 4in, is longer than some traditional 60 footers. The front deck has not been skimped either, allowing room for a four-person table to be used for picnics.

Certain elements of the plans of these boats were fixed while the remainder could be arranged to suit the owner's needs. The galley and bathroom were built to a standard layout and were located next to one another on the starboard side. At the rear, there were two single berths either side of the engine casing, which also formed the steps to the rear deck. In order to cram in the maximum amount of accommodation, these berths had their foot end under the rear deck.

Fabis has five berths, which was the maximum number possible. Stepping into the boat from the front deck, there are two 4ft-long benches, one on either side, that can be used as a four-person dinette or, with the table lowered, as a double bed across the boat. If fewer berths were required, this area was left open for two free-standing armchairs and a solid fuel stove.

Following this, on the starboard side, is a galley, which contains a fridge, an oven and a stainless steel worktop incorporating a hob, sink and drainer. To make more working space when the hob and sink are not needed, hinged lids can be lowered over them. Although the galley contains all the equipment you would expect to find in a narrowboat, it is all to a scale normally associated with glass fibre cruisers or small motor caravans.

On the port side, opposite the galley, there is a two-person dinette which can

Built and fitted out by Davison Brothers (not now trading)

Fabis has all the character of a much bigger boat.

Full review in
Waterways World
June 1978

convert to a single berth and has brackets above the four corners to support a pipe cot for very occasional use. Again, if fewer berths were needed, the dinette could be omitted and the space used for free-standing chairs.

Moving towards the rear, the starboard side has an enclosed bathroom containing a washbasin, Porta Potti type toilet and a shower tray with curtains. Using this cramped facility must demand the most extraordinary contortions even from the most lithe and fit members of the crew. A small, half height wardrobe occupies the opposite side before the two rear berths.

When a similar boat was reviewed in *Waterways World*, Michael Streat commented that personal privacy was non-existent and lack of stowage was a problem though he did give it nine out of ten for handling. Patricia Streat, on the other hand, reckoned that it was a boat that 'a family would get very fond of and which would be fun rather than work to cruise in'.

Top: The cabin looking rearwards. Note the cover over the galley units on the left.

Middle: Two benches can be used as a dinette or a double bed.

Right: The saloon and galley showing the combined hob and sink unit.

Bess

A 33ft narrowboat with a semi-traditional rear deck

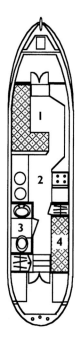

Bess

1 Saloon   7ft 6in
2 Galley   6ft 0in
3 Bathroom/
   locker   6ft 6in
4 Single berth

*B*ess was the first narrowboat I fitted out and an account of how I did it was published in *Waterways World* from September 1982 to January 1983. Its length of 33ft was determined partly by the length of our garden mooring and partly by what we thought we could afford at the time. The resulting cabin length of 20ft made planning very difficult but I accepted it as a challenge.

One feature of *Bess* which was unusual at the time – but quite common now – was the semi-traditional rear deck. We had looked at the advantages and disadvantages of traditional and cruiser sterns and could not make up our minds which to go for. While out cruising in our glass fibre cruiser, we encountered a boat built by Davison Brothers at Sawley which was, I believe, the first semi-traditional narrowboat ever built. I made a quick sketch of the layout and took it along to our chosen boatbuilder who said he could see no problems in incorporating this feature.

The design appeared to answer all our needs but, in practice, it did not perform as well as we hoped. There were fixed seats along each side but the cabin sides sloped in so much that we could never sit comfortably on them. Instead, we used to perch on the rather narrow handrails and use the seats as footrests. Also, although the boat may have looked traditional when viewed from the side, it lacked the extra internal space a proper traditional stern would have given.

The internal accommodation was divided into three parts. At the front, there was a small saloon with an L-shaped seat which was also used for dining and became our bed at night. It was about 7ft 6in in length which left just enough room at the foot of the bed for an angled shelf unit. In such a tight space, we felt there was not enough room to fit in a solid fuel stove safely so I installed a fan-assisted catalytic gas heater on the hull side opposite the seating. These units are no longer available so a diesel

Shell built by Stoke-on-Trent Boatbuilding (01782 813831)
Fitted out by the author

Bess showing the semi-traditional rear deck – novel then but commonplace now.

Full series in
Waterways World
September 1982
to January 1983

powered, warm air heating system would probably be the most suitable type of heating now.

The galley was basically an 'L' shape but, because it was so short, the bottom part of the 'L' was a four inch deep divider built onto the back of the seating in the saloon.

The last third of the layout also had a central corridor with the bathroom and a small clothes locker on one side, and a single berth and a wardrobe on the other. To save space in the bathroom, I used the integral shower tray solution. This served its purpose but meant that I had to lift the floor after every trip to mop up the inch of shower water that the sump pump always left. I made a removable upper bunk base which fitted above the single bed at gunwale level but we never used it.

Bess could be turned round in any reasonably wide stretch of canal and served us very well for five years. By this time, we had acquired a Labrador and realised we needed more space.

Above: The top mattress and base can be removed when not required.

Right (top): View from the front doors showing the saloon and galley.

Right (middle): The galley was big enough to produce a Christmas dinner.

Right (bottom): The author and his wife in the saloon. Note the raised divider between the galley and saloon.

Katsina and Little Gem

Two 38ft narrowboats with quite different approaches to design

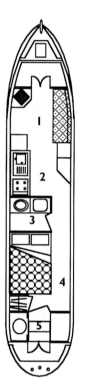
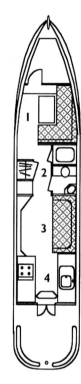

As I discovered with *Bess*, designing a shorter narrowboat calls for a ruthless streak to enable you to cut out all but the essentials. You then need a great deal of ingenuity to make the best use of what is left and fit it into the available space. *Katsina* and *Little Gem* are two 38ft boats that tackle the problem in quite different ways.

Katsina has a traditional shell and the plan is based on the 'floating cottage' layout described in Chapter Two. The saloon is 8ft long – just enough for a fixed seat with a small table unit at one end. The seat can be used as a single bed or pulled out to make a double.

The galley occupies the next

5ft 6in and has a continuous row of units on one side and an angled unit on the other to move the corridor from the centre to the starboard side. All the basic essentials – a fridge, cooker and sink unit – are fitted in although the worktop area is limited.

Space is saved in the bathroom by using the whole room as a shower cubicle and providing drainage slots in the floor, as I did on *Bess*, so it takes up only 4ft of valuable boat length.

Finally, there is a bedroom with a fixed double bed and a wardrobe. This accounts for about the same boat length as the saloon and, had it been built

Katsina

1	Saloon	8ft 0in
2	Galley	5ft 6in
3	Bathroom	4ft 0in
4	Bedroom	8ft 0in
5	Engine room	3ft 0in

Full review in *Waterways World*
January 1997

Little Gem

1	Bedroom	6ft 6in
2	Toilet/shower	6ft 0in
3	Saloon	7ft 0in
4	Galley	5ft 6in

Featured in *Waterways World*
May 2002

Katsina

Shell and fit out by
Stoke on Trent
Boatbuilding Co
(01782 813831)

Little Gem

Shell and fit out by
Midland Canal Centre
01283 701933
Sold through
Sawley Marina
(0115 973 4278)

as a convertible dinette, would have added about 40% to the day space on the boat. The engine is tucked under the steps leading to the rear deck. These are designed to be easily removable for access. To one side of the steps are the batteries and, to the other, the calorifier.

Little Gem is the same length but has a cruiser stern and the layout is capable of being altered to suit the individual owners' needs. At the rear of the cabin is a through galley, again with all the essentials but more worktops. Next, there is a small midships saloon which could be furnished with two chairs, a settee or a settee that converts to a double bed. On the opposite side is a shelf unit that widens at one end to take a TV.

Moving forward there are separate toilet and shower compartments for maximum flexibility of use. Opposite these is a wardrobe and a floor-to-ceiling shelf unit.

At the front of the cabin, there is another small cabin that could contain a fixed double bed or an L-shaped dinette that can convert to a double bed. The boat is heated by a small diesel boiler supplying two radiators and a calorifier for hot water.

Little Gem (pictures right)
Top: The midships saloon.
Middle: More worktop space in the through galley.
Bottom: The front cabin showing the double bed option.

Katsina (pictures left)
Top: The bathroom takes up only four feet of boat length.
Middle: The galley looking through to the saloon.
Bottom left: A fixed double bed in the bedroom.
Bottom right: The rear steps are removable for access to the engine.

Albion

40ft traditional narrowboat with a multi-purpose hold

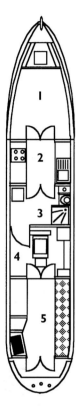

The minimum recommended length for a boat with all the usual facilities and a traditional engine room and back cabin is 62ft. This can be reduced to 56ft if you are prepared to dispense with the bedroom and sleep in the back cabin but trying to plan a fully traditional 40ft boat required the owners of *Albion* to do some really radical thinking.

By the time they had added the foredeck, engine room and back cabin to their 40ft outline plan, they had only 17ft for the remainder of the accommodation. The first 4ft in front of the engine room are taken up by a walk-through bathroom with a small corner shower compartment, a basin and a diesel boiler. Next comes a 5ft through-galley, containing cooker, fridge and sink unit, which leaves about 8ft before the start of the foredeck. This could have been used for a small saloon cabin with, perhaps, fixed side benches and a stove at one end but it would have made *Albion* look like

what it was – a small narrowboat.

They decided instead to have a multi-purpose hold covered only by cloths supported by a cratch and top plank. In the spring and autumn, they eat and sleep in the back cabin but, in warmer weather, the cloths are rolled up and they can enjoy al fresco meals or simply lounge in the sun at the front. The floor level in the galley is continued through into the hold so that it feels and functions more like a part of the interior.

The steel gunwales either side of the hold are lowered to allow thick mahogany cappings to be fixed to them. These provide a more pleasant surface to lean on or step onto and make it much easier to attach the fixings for the substantial black, acrylic canvas cover.

One item on the wish list for the shell was a full traditional forecabin but the owners soon realised that it would look out of place on a boat of this length. They went instead for a scaled down version

Shell built by G & J Reeves (01926 815581)
Fitted out by the owner

1 Multi-purpose
   deck   8ft 0in
2 Galley   5ft 0in
3 Bathroom   4ft 0in
4 Engine room 5ft 0in
5 Back cabin 8ft 6in

Albion showing the small forecabin for the gas bottles.

Full review in
Waterways World
March 1998

with gas locker above and a useful deck gear locker, accessible from the front deck space, below.

Since half the cabin accommodation consists of the back cabin and engine room, the owners decided to continue the scumble treatment through the rest of the boat.

The meaty proportions of the front and rear deck mean that, should the present or future owners decide that they really need some more space, the boat could be lengthened very successfully. In its present form, *Albion* proves that there is no reason why a boat that, by normal standards would be considered short, should look out of place when rubbing shoulders with full length boats.

Left: Good access to the weed hatch from the rear deck.

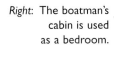

Right: The boatman's cabin is used as a bedroom.

Left: Washbasin and the drip-feed diesel stove in the bathroom.

Right: Looking towards the hold from the through-galley.

Below: The multi-purpose deck. Note the timber gunwales.

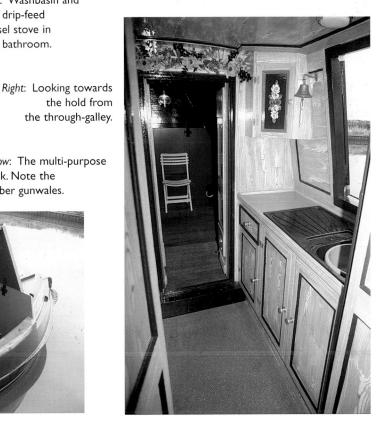

Petula

A 53ft cruiser-style narrowboat with rear galley and forward bedroom

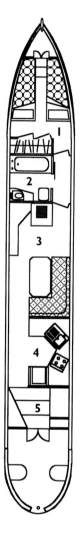

A large cruiser deck may not be as popular with private boaters as a traditional stern but it does allow the whole crew to come together for cruising or relaxing. Having included one large outside space, there seemed little reason for another so *Petula*'s owners decided to dispense with the front well deck, allowing more room inside. They also reckoned that a closed front deck would be more suitable for occasional trips down the Severn to Bristol or across the Wash. With these decisions made, it seemed logical to reverse the conventional plan and have the day accommodation towards the rear and the sleeping area at the front.

From the centrally placed rear doors, a flight of steps passes at an angle through a lobby area with a drying cabinet to one side. On the opposite side are ledges with bean bags for the owner's dogs. The main central area of the plan is occupied by the galley and saloon.

U-shaped galleys make a good refuge for the cook when the rest of the crew needs to pass but they generally contain two difficult-to-get-at corners. The owner has overcome this problem by making the base of the 'U' into a 'V' so that the corner units have larger doors giving much easier access. The hob and sink are set at the same angles, which gives a more interesting appearance to the whole galley.

Fixed seating in narrowboats almost invariably comprises flat seats and, sometimes, vertical backs which become uncomfortable after a short time. The dinette on *Petula* has seats that slope upwards towards the front and backrests that hinge down from their inclined position to form a horizontal base when a bed is required. The space behind the backrest is used to store spare table tops with Desmo leg sockets. The table tops also make up the missing part of the bed base.

Shell built by Pickwell & Arnold (01706 812411)
Fitted out by the owner

1	Bedroom	10ft 0in
2	Bathroom	5ft 0in
3	Saloon	12ft 0in
4	Galley	7ft 6in
5	Lobby	4ft 6in

Petula showing the small foredeck.

Full review in
Waterways World
August 2000

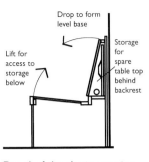

Moving forward, there is a bathroom on the port side and, finally, a bedroom with a small pair of outward opening doors for escape. The bedroom has single berths to each side but these can be converted to a king size double by pulling out a 'train' of battens, joined by webbing, from the far end of the gap. These form a base for a loose foam cushion stored under the front deck.

To increase the feeling of spaciousness, there is a generous internal headroom of 6ft 7in – achieved partly by using a thicker base plate, which reduces the amount of ballast needed. Higher than usual gunwales also contribute by increasing the part of the interior that enjoys maximum width but this advantage is gained at the expense of higher window sills which limit views from the boat.

Detail of the sloping seating.

Right (top): The small front doors of this forward bedroom are for escape.

Right (middle): A train of battens fills the gap between the two berths.

Right (bottom): The saloon and galley form a large central space.

Left (top): Angled hob and sink.

Left (bottom): Solid fuel stove and useful shelves in the saloon.

Dispatch and Uranus

Two traditional narrowboats of 52ft 6in and 55ft with interesting planning features

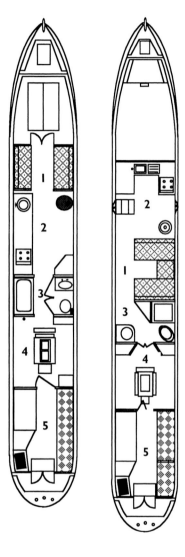

Dispatch and *Uranus* have been included as much for the interesting and imaginative way in which parts of their interiors have been designed as for the way in which the whole layout has been planned. Both have long tug-like front decks although one is raised and the other slightly lowered. They also have traditional boatman's cabins which, in order to allow sufficient space for other accommodation further forward, are both used as the main sleeping area.

The first area in front of the engine room in both boats is a through bathroom. In *Uranus*, the circulation path moves to the port side, leaving three corners which are occupied by a shower cubicle, an angled toilet and a washbasin that resembles a ceramic bowl on a shelf. The

bathroom on *Dispatch* is bisected by a central corridor. On one side is a wash basin and toilet which are enclosed by double doors so that they can be used without restricting passage through the boat. The doors can be opened across the corridor to form a large space when the bath, on the opposite side of the corridor, is needed. When not in use, the bath is covered by an upholstered seat and becomes an attractive alcove.

Having moved the corridor to one side, *Uranus* now has a U-shaped dinette which also serves as the saloon seating. Instead of the usual loose table top supported on a Desmo leg, a hinged panel is lowered from the cabin side and is supported on a chain from the roof when a table is required. The galley is also 'U' shaped but, because the

An unusually deep draught gives *Dispatch* a long, low look.

Dispatch
Shell built by Tim Tyler (01889 271414)
Fitted out by Braidbar Boats (01625 873471)

Lack of portholes gives scope for some seriously bold signwriting.

Uranus
Shell and fit out by Stowe Hill Marine (01327 431365)

	Dispatch	Uranus
1 Saloon	4ft 6in	8ft 6in
2 Galley	9ft 0in	6ft 0in
3 Bathroom	4ft 6in	4ft 6in
4 Engine room	8ft 0in	7ft 0in
5 Boatman's cabin	8ft 6in	9ft 0in
Full review in	July	July
Waterways World	1999	2001

front bulkhead has no doors in it, it is arranged across the front of the cabin and not to one side. This, together with the absence of portholes in the cabin sides, allows far more wall cupboards than normal to be accommodated to very good effect.

The galley on *Dispatch* occupies one side of the central corridor, the other side being an open area with a corner cupboard at one end and a solid fuel stove at the other. Opening up the plan in this way greatly reduces the tunnel effect normally associated with a central corridor. At the front of the cabin is a pair of fixed seats, facing one another, which can be used for dining or converted to a double bed for occasional use.

Both boats make great use of paint for the interior finishes. *Uranus* compensates for its lack of portholes with large 'dog boxes' or roof lights but the amount of light these give is still limited. To make as much use of the light as possible, the cabin sides and ceiling are painted cream, which combines with the waxed oak woodwork to give a very pleasant farmhouse character.

The interior of *Dispatch* makes much use of reclaimed materials and furniture parts to create a deliberately well worn effect. This is enhanced by the finish, which is similar to scumbling except that the base coat is white emulsion with a mixture of blue green gloss and white spirit applied sparingly over it. The cabin sides and ceiling are painted, equally sparingly, in cream.

Dispatch (pictures above)
Top: The central corridor becomes an open area as it passes through the galley.
Middle: Subtly applied finishes give the furniture a well worn appearance.
Bottom: The bath forms an attractive alcove seat when not in use.

Uranus (pictures right)
Top: The U-shaped galley is located across the front of the cabin.
Middle: The dinette arranged for dining …
Bottom: … and for lounging.

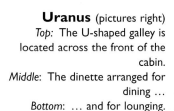

Kalikamara

A 54ft traditional-style narrowboat with the classic 'floating cottage' plan

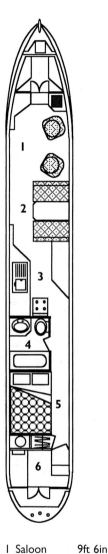

The term 'floating cottage' is used so much that you may be forgiven for thinking that it refers to a rather stale or hackneyed layout. However, this would be a great injustice for, as I pointed out in Chapter Two, the reason there are so many boats with this plan is because it works so well. Also, because they are likely to have a wider appeal, 'floating cottages' tend to sell more easily when the time comes.

The basic layout, consisting of saloon, galley, bathroom and bedroom, can be used on boats from 36ft up to 70ft long but it is normally associated with lengths ranging from 48ft to 60ft. At 54ft, *Kalikamara* is well within this and so warrants a closer examination.

One of the requirements of a floating cottage is that it should be easy for two people to manage but capable of accommodating two guests in reasonable privacy for occasional weekends. On shorter examples, these guests generally sleep on a bed/settee in the saloon but, if the boat is towards the upper end of the popular range, a convertible dinette can be included as it has on *Kalikamara*. This leaves a saloon area about 9ft 6ins long which is just big enough to take two free-standing chairs, a solid fuel stove and a TV cupboard.

A saloon of this size would normally feel rather cramped but, as the dinette is adjacent to it, the two spaces combine to form one large day area. A small refinement might have been to have an L-shaped dinette that would have presented an open face to the saloon and made a more usable single space.

On boats of 60ft and over, more boat length can be allocated to the saloon part, which gives the option of placing the dinette between the galley and bathroom. One advantage of doing this is that it allows two groups to pursue different activities like playing cards and watching television.

Shell built and fitted out by Alvechurch Boat Centres (0121 445 2909)

Kalikamara.

1 Saloon	9ft 6in
2 Dinette	6ft 6in
3 Galley	8ft 0in
4 Bathroom	5ft 9in
5 Bedroom	8ft 0in
6 Engine room	4ft 0in

Full review in
Waterways World
January 2002

The galley which follows is the 'double L' type, allowing the corridor to pass from the port to starboard side and avoiding the 'railway carriage effect'. To assist the flow of circulation through the galley, the end floor units are triangular rather than square.

A small conventionally planned bathroom is next and has a small flap at low level in the corridor wall to allow the cassette to be removed from under the toilet. It is in the bedroom that most of the economies in planning have been made. The bed has been built in on three sides with an airing cupboard over the hot water cylinder, accessible over the foot of the bed.

Externally, *Kalikamara* has a rather short foredeck for a boat of this size which, taken with the planning economies seen in the bedroom, suggest that this particular plan might have benefited from two or three extra feet of boat length. This apart, the boat has a pleasant feel and is much enjoyed by its owners.

Right (top): The dinette between the galley and saloon.
Right (middle): The saloon looking towards the front deck.
Right (bottom): The corridor switches from one side to the other in the galley.

Left: Fixed double bed with cupboards and lighting above.

Bottom left: Spare cassettes are stored in the base of the vanity unit.
Bottom middle: Storage under the dinette is accessible from the saloon.

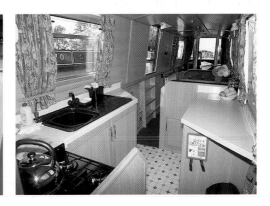

Free Spirit

A 55ft cruiser-style narrowboat with midships saloon and a multi-purpose cabin

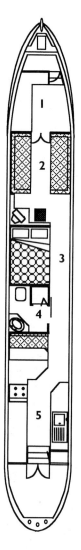

Like the owners of *Petula*, *Free Spirit*'s owners considered taking a 'floating cottage' plan and simply turning it round so that the saloon was next to the cruiser rear deck. However, this did not really suit their requirements so they started with a blank sheet of paper and came up with a very personal layout.

Their first decision was to place the galley at the back so that it acts as a lobby where wet clothes can be removed when entering the cabin. Two work tops flank a central corridor for the first few feet before an L-shaped unit with a glazed cupboard above diverts it to the starboard side. To emphasise the galley's role as a gathering place, there is a fixed, rearward facing bench and a hinged flap which can be raised for twosome meals.

A conventional bathroom with a space-saving sliding door is followed by a fairly minimal bedroom containing a fixed double bed and cupboards over each end. The space under the bed has sliding drawers for storage.

Next comes the midships saloon with a natural draught oil-fired stove on the centre line of the boat forming a strong focus and giving a more domestic feel to the area. Beside it is a cupboard and shelf unit for the television. The rest of the saloon is furnished with two fixed benches. These can be converted to form a double bed across the boat.

At the front of the boat there is a small cabin which could be used for hobbies and has a slatted side bench which converts to a further double bed if required. An offset front door leads to the tiny well deck but the owners say that, if they could turn the clock back, they would dispense with this deck and simply have an escape hatch onto the foredeck.

The whole interior is lined in T&G pine and similarly coloured plywood.

Shell built by Liverpool Boats   (0151 707 0722)
Fitted out by the owner

Free Spirit.

1 Front cabin 6ft 6in
2 Saloon   10ft 0in
3 Bedroom   6ft 6in
4 Bathroom   5ft 6in
5 Galley/
   dinette   13ft 6in

Full review in
Waterways World
April 2001

Teamed with a russet and gold material for all the curtains and upholstery throughout the boat, this creates a very warm, unified effect.

Looking at the downsides first, all the sleeping areas are on the same side of the bathroom. This could be improved by transposing the bedroom and bathroom to give independent access. There is also very little clothes storage space in the rather tight bedroom.

However, all these are more than offset by the well balanced circulation path that gives interesting views as you walk through the boat. The galley/dinette works well as an informal day area that has good contact with the rear deck. The saloon is also very successful with what appear to be two settees facing one another in front of the centrally placed stove in true cottage style. The space taken up by the front cabin could have been used to make the other areas larger but it has many possible uses and the owners feel it is worth having.

Top (left and right): This bench in the front cabin converts to a double bed.

Right: A homely feel in the saloon.

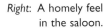

Left: The L-shaped galley as seen from the dinette.

Left: Room divider between the galley and two-person dinette.

Right: Two fixed seats with upholstery to match the curtains.

Caie Too

A 57ft traditional style narrowboat with convertible dinette and a cross bed

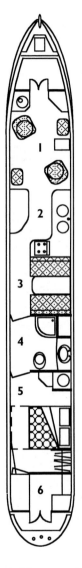

Caie Too is based on a go-anywhere 57ft traditional shell with a fairly short front deck and no cratch, but its relatively unexceptional exterior conceals an interior that has many interesting features.

The saloon has a stove and TV cabinet either side of the front doors and is furnished with two leather recliners and some small pieces of free-standing furniture. At the far end is the L-shaped galley entered from the centre. A circular stainless steel sink and drainer are set in the laminated timber worktop and the veneer faced doors below open to reveal cupboards, a 230-volt fridge and a washing machine. As well as having rounded corners to the worktops, the sides and ends are subtly curved rather than dead straight to give a more interesting appearance.

Next comes a dinette that converts to a double bed for occasional visitors before a side door leads you to a through bathroom. Here, the woodwork is as curvaceous as in the galley and this theme is reinforced by the quadrant shaped shower cubicle. The cabin side is covered by mirror glass with a porthole let into the centre.

The bedroom, which follows, occupies 11ft of boat length – nine inches more than the saloon – and has a double bed across the boat. At night, the foot end of the bed telescopes out to support the mattress extension over the corridor. Turning the bed across the boat allows room for a bedside table unit on one side and a generous wardrobe on the other. Finally, another side door leads to a small engine room.

Caie Too is lined in panels of cherry with frames and furniture in walnut, both gloss finished and set off by chrome, rather than brass, fittings. The ceiling consists of cream painted panels, routed

Shell built by Jonathan Wilson (01142 786490)
Fitted out by Roger Myers (01625 575811)

Caie Too.

1 Saloon	10ft 3in
2 Galley	7ft 6in
3 Dinette	6ft 6in
4 Bathroom	6ft 0in
5 Bedroom	11ft 0in
6 Engine room	4ft 6in

Full review in
Waterways World
February 2003

to suggest tiles, into which are set the downlighters that provide the majority of the lighting onboard. Looking down, two different types of timber are used to form a geometric design in the laminated flooring. Curtains cover the saloon windows but, in the rest of the boat, stainless steel slatted blinds are used.

In an interior where style is such a strong consideration, it is good to see that practical considerations have not been forgotten. The laminate floor panels are fixed in a way that allows them to be removed for access to a hatch in the ply floor boarding beneath and the ceiling panels can be removed just as easily to get to wiring and service the light fittings. In the bedroom, a seemingly fixed triangular unit can be moved aside so that the calorifier in the cupboard behind can be checked.

Right (top): Turning the bed creates space for a bedside table and cupboard.

Right (middle): Rich wood tones in the dinette.

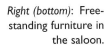

Right (bottom): Free-standing furniture in the saloon.

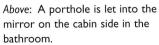

Above: A porthole is let into the mirror on the cabin side in the bathroom.

Below: Even the straight lines are curved in the galley.

Merlin and Scythia

Two 57ft traditional narrowboats with boatman's cabins and
engine rooms but different layouts forward

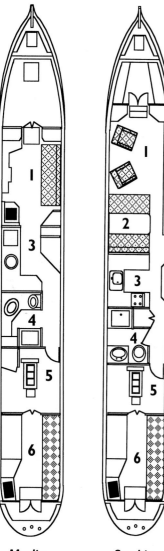

Merlin and *Scythia* are both 57ft traditional narrowboats with boatman's cabins and engine rooms and, coincidentally, won awards at the 2002 IWA Festival. Both owners wanted to limit the length of their boat to 57ft to enable them to cruise the northern canals. *Scythia's* owners originally planned to have an engine room at the rear to leave space for a fixed double bed but decided at the last minute that they really wanted a boatman's cabin so they opted to dispense with the bedroom and sleep in the dropdown bed of the boatman's cabin. *Merlin's* owners had made this decision from the start.

In spite of their obvious similarities, it is interesting to see how some slight changes to the planning and overall dimensions have enabled one to have an extra area of accommodation.

The two boatman's cabins are almost identical in length but the engine room of *Scythia*, which contains a Beta Tug engine, is 5ft long whereas *Merlin's*, with its Lister JP2, measures 7ft 9in.

The bathrooms, which follow, are about the same length, although *Scythia* manages to squeeze in a cupboard off the corridor while *Merlin* uses the space for a larger vanity unit. *Merlin's* galley is 'L' shaped, which brings the corridor from

Merlin *(left)* showing the long tug deck.

Shell built by Jonathan Wilson (01142 786490) Fitted out by the owner

Merlin		Scythia
10ft 6in	1 Saloon	10ft 0in
–	2 Dinette	6ft 6in
7ft 6in	3 Galley	6ft 6in
5ft 6in	4 Bathroom	5ft 6in
7ft 9in	5 Engine room	5ft 0in
9ft 0in	6 Boatman's cabin	9ft 0in

Full reviews of both boats
Waterways World December 2002

Scythia *(right)* has a well deck.

Shell built and fitted out by S M Hudson Boat Builders (01827 311317)

the starboard side to the centre where it enters the saloon, and is 7ft 6in long. *Scythia's* galley is a tighter 6ft 6in and is 'U' shaped, leaving the corridor on the same side.

This allows *Scythia's* owners to incorporate a 6ft 6in dinette that converts to an occasional double bed. The dinette has no backrest at the forward end so that the seat can be used as part of the 10ft saloon at the front of the cabin. *Merlin's* saloon is only 6 inches longer and has a fixed seat that also converts to a double bed and a boatman's cabin inspired table cupboard.

The differences continue at the front of the boats where *Scythia* has a relatively generous 5ft well deck and 6ft foredeck but *Merlin* uses some of the length saved by dispensing with a dinette to have a 7ft raised tug deck and a 6ft foredeck. This gives the boat more of a traditional tug-like appearance, although the steps into the saloon are taller and a sliding hatch is added over the doors to make entry and exit easier.

In *Merlin*, the scumbled finish in the boatman's cabin is continued throughout the interior, whereas there is a complete contrast between the materials used in the 'old' and 'new' parts of *Scythia*. The two boats demonstrate that a few subtle changes can make a difference not only to the amount of accommodation but also to the overall character of the boat.

Merlin (pictures left)
Top: Details associated with the boatman's cabin are used throughout the interior.
Middle: Scumbled surfaces combined with cream panels lighten the bathroom.
Bottom: The L-shaped galley looking towards the saloon.

Scythia (pictures right)
Top: After a late change of plan the boatman's cabin is used as a bedroom.
Middle: More modern finishes are used in the forward accommodation.
Bottom: The saloon and dinette. Note the lack of a backrest.

Biding Time

A 58ft traditional-style narrowboat with an unconventional plan

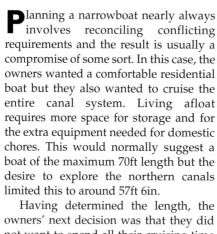

Planning a narrowboat nearly always involves reconciling conflicting requirements and the result is usually a compromise of some sort. In this case, the owners wanted a comfortable residential boat but they also wanted to cruise the entire canal system. Living afloat requires more space for storage and for the extra equipment needed for domestic chores. This would normally suggest a boat of the maximum 70ft length but the desire to explore the northern canals limited this to around 57ft 6in.

Having determined the length, the owners' next decision was that they did not want to spend all their cruising time at opposite ends of the boat so, rather than locate the saloon at the front where it is on many traditional boats, they opted to turn the plan around and have the bedroom there.

Entering the cabin through the front doors, there is a landing with a flight of steps leading down to one side. This device certainly lends style but is rather wasteful of space so its use on a boat where storage space is at a premium is questionable. Nevertheless, the bedroom is a pleasant and quite private area.

Moving rearwards, there is a through bathroom containing a large corner bath, a vanity unit and a toilet. It has Brazilian cedar boarding on the walls and floor, which gives it the character of a sauna.

A deep archway leads from the bathroom into the saloon, which is at the heart of the boat. The front part of the saloon is furnished with two leather recliners while the rear half has a fixed L-shaped dinette. This is more open than the type with two opposing benches and so can be used as occasional seating without half of the occupants having their backs to the saloon. If it had been built slightly longer, it could have been converted to a double berth but the owners were keen to preserve the two person status of the boat.

Halfway along the cabin side of the combined saloon and dining area there is

Shell built by Jonathan Wilson (01142 786490)
Fitted out by Fernwood Craft (01476 860440)

Biding Time.

1	Bedroom	10ft 6ins
2	Bathroom	8ft 0ins
3	Saloon/ dinette	16ft 0ins
4	Galley	8ft 0ins
5	Engine room	3ft 6ins

Full review in
Waterways World
July 2001

a solid fuel stove with shelves above and to either side. This create a strong feature, pulling the two spaces together. There is also a pair of side doors to provide more light and air to the otherwise portholed interior.

The rear galley is somewhere between a straight through and an L-shaped type with two 45° offsets to ease passage through it. Cooking equipment is all electric on this gasless boat and is smaller than usual to reflect the owners' intention to take generous advantage of canalside restaurants.

A pair of double doors lead from the galley to the engine room which also contains a 7kW generator (larger cooking appliances would have required something in excess of 10kW), an inverter and a very limited amount of storage.

The owners of *Biding Time* had had little boating experience when they commissioned it and this enabled them to approach the design with few pre-conceptions. Working with the builder, they produced a very interesting layout that would be ideal for cruising at all times of the year. However, if used as a permanent residential boat, the limited amount of storage space would call for self discipline of a high order.

Top (left): Solid fuel stove and shelves create a strong feature in the saloon.
Top (centre): The non-convertible dinette.
Top (right): The all-electric galley.

Right: Front steps are stylish but rather wasteful of space.

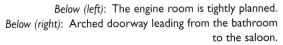

Below (left): The engine room is tightly planned.
Below (right): Arched doorway leading from the bathroom to the saloon.

Left: Vertical T&G combine with diagonal floor boards to give a sauna effect.

Lady Selina

A 58ft 6in cruiser-style narrowboat, considerably modified by its owners

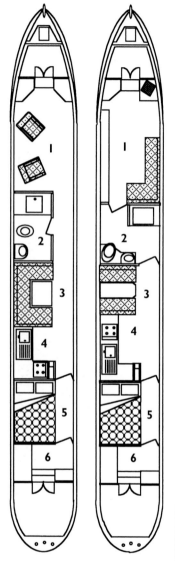

As previous reviews have shown. different layouts can alter the appearance of two similar boats but, in *Lady Selina*, this can be demonstrated in the same boat. It also shows that, in order to have a 'new' boat, you do not always have to start with a new shell.

The owners bought *Lady Selina* second-hand and were quite happy with it to begin with. However, after they had cruised it for a while, they discovered that the galley was on the small side for family meals and, conversely, the bathroom seemed to take up more of the boat's length than was necessary. Also, since all this accommodation was on the same side of the boat, it left a long, boring corridor down the other side.

Their first move was to measure the spaces and furniture and note which parts of the fit out could be moved easily and which would require more upheaval. Using this information, they produced a plan on a computer. This enabled them to move the remaining partitions and

fittings around easily and see what improvements might be possible.

The partition between the bathroom and the dinette was the most difficult to move so they used this as a base point. To the rear of it, the owners decided to reduce the size of the dinette and give the space gained to the galley. This means that the dinette can no longer be converted to a double bed but, as we shall see, they managed to include this facility in another part of the boat. The basic 'L' shape of the galley and the position of the Alde boiler are retained but all the other fittings and equipment have been replaced.

It seemed that the best way to break up the continuous side corridor and to give more space to the saloon was to create a through bathroom with doors in diagonally opposite corners. By doing this, they now have a bathroom which feels more spacious and yet takes up less boat length than the old one.

In its previous form, the saloon

Shell built by Tayberg Steel Boats (01484 400221)
Fitted out by the owner

Lady Selina's cruiser deck.

Before	After
1 Saloon	14ft 0in
2 Bathroom	6ft 0in
3 Dinette	5ft 6in
4 Galley	7ft 6in
5 Bedroom	6ft 6in
6 Lobby	4ft 0in

Full review in
Waterways World
February 2002

had free-standing furniture but the owner opted for a fixed, 'L' shaped seating unit that converts to a double bed. As well as making up for the loss of the dinette as a second sleeping area, this has the advantage of being on the right side of the bathroom to allow independent access at night. Moving from free-standing to fixed seating is against the normal trend but there is space in the enlarged saloon for a chair if required. Opposite the seating unit, there is a useful run of under-gunwale shelves while a pine corner unit and a solid fuel stove flank the front doors.

With these modifications, the owners achieved their objectives and enjoy their boat far more.

Left: A smaller dinette allows more space for the galley.

Below: Shelves and the L-shaped seating in the saloon.

Right (top): White units brighten up the galley.

Right (middle): The enlarged saloon with bathroom beyond.

Right (bottom): The new through bathroom as seen from the saloon.

Sammy Jo

A 60ft traditional narrowboat with ideas developed from a previous boat

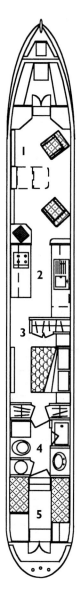

The owners of *Sammy Jo* had owned a 60ft semi-traditional narrowboat with the classic 'floating cottage' layout similar to *Kalikamara*. However, having an extra 6ft of overall length and an L-shaped dinette between the saloon and galley, the boat felt very spacious. It suited the owners well but, when they retired, they had to decide whether to modify the boat to their changed requirements or to sell it and build anew. They went for the latter and commissioned a similar length boat from the same builder, but with a completely different layout.

The main external difference between the two boats was a switch from a semi-traditional rear deck which, when the first boat was built, made an ideal playpen for their grandchildren. This was changed to a traditional stern to accommodate the generator necessary for all the domestic equipment they needed for extended cruising.

A cratch still covers the front deck and,

moving inside, the saloon is still at the front of the new boat. The TV cabinet occupies a corner by the side of the front doors as it did before but the solid fuel stove is at the rear of the saloon, next to the galley where its warmth is more widely felt. There is no dinette and two large leather chairs dominate the space. At mealtimes, a hinged flap, incorporated into a run of shelving along the hull side, lifts up and a further flap and supporting leg unfold to form a dining table.

A central corridor through the galley gives the maximum number of units in the given space and, in a two-person boat, creates few bottleneck conflicts. Although the 6.5kW generator would permit limited electric cooking, the owners opted for a gas hob and oven backed up by a microwave oven.

The occasional sleeping accommodation is moved from the front of the boat to the back so the bedroom and bathroom are transposed. The bedroom has a thwartships double bed and is lit by a

Shell built by Marque Narrowboats (Not now trading)
Fitted out by Stephen Goldsbrough Boats (01564 778210)

Sammy Jo the second.

1 Saloon   15ft 0ins
2 Galley   8ft 0ins
3 Bedroom   11ft 0ins
4 Bathroom   6ft 0ins
5 Rear cabin   7ft 0ins

Full review in
Waterways World
January 2000

roof light and two portholes, making it feel very private. Generous wardrobe provision is further evidence of the semi-residential specification.

Next comes what might be described as a through bathroom although, with both doors placed centrally and the washing machine in one corner, it has more the feel of a corridor with fittings on either side. At night, and with the doors closed, it is probably quite different but, in daylight hours, it lacks the relaxing character of its forebear.

Finally, the plan steps up to a platform over the engine and the generator. Foam cushions can be arranged on the platform to make an occasional bed for visitors.

With their first boat, the owners sensibly opted for a tried and tested layout but changing requirements and a few more years experience have given them the opportunity to design a more personal boat for extended cruising.

Top (lef)t: The bathroom is bisected by a through corridor.

Top (right): Cushions can be arranged over the engine casing to form a bed.

Below: The stove is now between the saloon and galley.

Right: Secluded bedroom with thwartships double bed.

Right: The dining table folds out from the hull side shelves.

Below: The more conventional saloon and dinette of *Sammy Jo 1*.

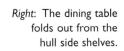

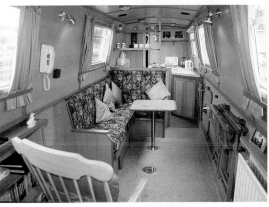

Footsie 100

A 60ft 'semi-cruiser' style narrowboat with an unusual plan and some novel features

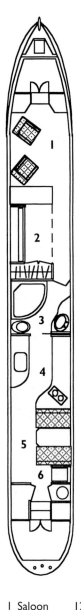

Like the previous boat, *Footsie 100* was commissioned by a couple who had just retired and wanted a boat that was suitable for extended cruising and that could accommodate occasional guests.

Internally, the layout starts fairly conventionally with a two-person saloon containing leather recliners and a gravity fed diesel stove. This is divided from the next area by a double-sided peninsular unit with cupboards on one side and a knee-hole desk on the other

The space that follows is the most innovative for, by day, it is a study or an extension to the saloon while, at night, it becomes the main bedroom. The owners see no problem in spending a few minutes each morning and evening folding away and setting up the bed if it means that they have 7ft of addition space all through the day. The bed is housed in a cupboard to one side and drops down to form a 4ft 6ins wide, lengthways bed – the owner is too tall for the more traditional crossways solution.

At the centre of the plan, a through bathroom takes the corridor from the starboard to the centre where it enters the galley. It contains a large corner bath and a vanity unit on the opposite side.

The galley is basically 'L' shaped but has smooth, flowing lines which lead the eye on through the boat. All the cooking equipment is electric and includes a two ring induction hob that only gets hot if a pan is placed on it. Adjacent to the galley is a raised dinette which, together with the galley, forms a totally separate day space.

At the very back is the 'business' end of the boat where the engine, 7kW generator, inverter/charger, air conditioning unit and a washing machine are housed in an engine room-cum-utility area. All of these items are tucked away unobtrusively and over the washing machine there is a flap that allows access to the controls when needed but makes a neat, flush wall when they are not.

Shell built by Midland Canal Centre 01283 701933
Fitted out by Stephen Goldsbrough Boats 01564 778210

Footsie 100 showing the 'semi cruiser' rear deck.

1 Saloon   12ft 0in
2 Bedroom   9ft 0in
3 Bathroom   6ft 0in
4 Galley   8ft 0in
5 Dinette   6ft 6in
6 Utility/engine
   room   6ft 0in

Full review in
Waterways World
December 2001

Being gasless means that *Footsie 100* does not need a gas locker and this has allowed fixed seating to be taken around the front deck almost to the stem post

and there is a guardrail-cum-backrest all round. At the rear, there is a longish, flat rear deck which, it has been suggested, is not so much semi-traditional as semi-cruiser and gives ample room for two or three people while preserving modestly traditional lines. To keep the steerer's feet from freezing on winter cruises, warm air is ducted from the engine bay beneath through vents around the edge.

The unusual bedroom on *Footsie 100* means that the entire length of the boat is usable during the daytime although it should be remembered that the thickness of the mattress and the inward slope of the cabin side limit the area in front of the bed to about two thirds of the width of the boat.

Right: Gentle curving lines in the galley.

Below: *(Top)* The bedroom/study in day … and *(bottom)* night modes.

Bottom right: The dinette looking towards the rear deck.

Top (left): Seating all around the front deck.
Top (right): Freestanding furniture in the saloon.

Rome and Lady Ebrington

Two similar 60ft traditional boats, one with a modified saloon and the other with a variation in the galley and bedroom

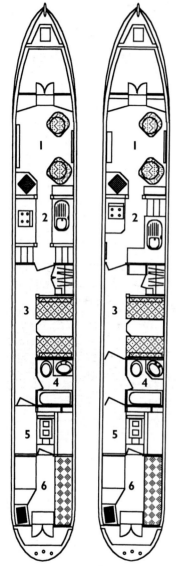

Rome is the third boat I fitted out for ourselves and the story of how I did this is told in the *Narrowboat Builders' Book*. It is designed as a two-person boat with the possibility of accommodating guests in the boatman's cabin. The bathroom is located between the boatman's cabin and the dinette, which converts to a double bed at night. I recognised that within the 60ft length, all the remaining spaces would be rather tight so I opted for a through galley, which gave the greatest amount of storage in the minimum length.

When it came to the saloon, I decided to have three fixed single seats in the corners, the fourth corner being occupied by a solid fuel stove. This left a reasonably sized space in the middle, which made the saloon feel bigger. Unfortunately the fixed seats were not very comfortable, especially during long autumn evenings, and there was no permanent place for a television or hi-fi system to take our minds off the seats.

Since the rest of the boat suited us very well, I decided to remove the fixed seats, build shelf units for the TV and hi-fi either side of the front doors and buy two leather recliner chairs. This has transformed the whole boat and has greatly increased our enjoyment of cruising it.

Shortly after I fitted out *Rome*, I was asked to fit out another 60 footer, *Lady Ebrington*, on similar lines but with one or two variations.

Rome
Shell built by Les Allen and Sons (not now trading)
Fitted out by the author

Lady Ebrington
Shell built by Colecraft (01926 814081)
Fitted out by the author.

The traditional lines of *Rome*.

Rome (left) and
Lady Ebrington (right)

1 Saloon	11ft 6in
2 Galley (inc side steps)	7ft 0in
3 Bedroom/dinette	9ft 6in
4 Bathroom	6ft 0in
5 Engine room	5ft 0in
6 Boatman's cabin	8ft 0in

Rome is fully described in the Narrowboat Builders' Book.

Most of the changes took place in the galley, which would have to cater for a larger crew than ours so more worktop space was needed. Since the accommodation on either side of the galley was fixed in size, the additional space had to be found from within. The solution was to dispense with one of the raked steps leading to the side doors and substitute a vertical ladder that could be located in a side corridor.

The galley is 'L' shaped and entered from the saloon through a triple-arched divider. On the starboard side, adjacent to the divider, I positioned one raking flight of steps with built in storage. Moving the corridor over to the port side as it enters the bedroom gave the opportunity for a Welsh dresser-style fitting on the rear bulkhead of the galley. It also gave more space in front of the wardrobe in the bedroom so I was able to incorporate a full height bookshelf unit with a drop-down writing flap. In the bathroom, the basin was turned through 45° and the vanity unit given a more Victorian look.

These few changes, plus a switch from oak framing and wallpaper panels to pine framing and cream painted panels, gave what was basically an identical boat, a completely different character.

Rome (pictures left)
Top: The saloon as originally planned ...

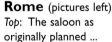

Middle: ... and with new free-standing furniture.

Bottom: The galley looking through the central door to the bedroom.

Lady Ebrington
(pictures right)
Top: The modified galley has more worktop space but one flight of steps is replaced by a ladder.
Middle: Moving the corridor to one side makes room for an extra bookshelf unit in the bedroom. (The dinette table has been lowered to bed mode).
Bottom: It also allowed space for a Welsh dresser in the galley.

Rose

A 67ft narrowboat with a semi-traditional rear deck and a central corridor

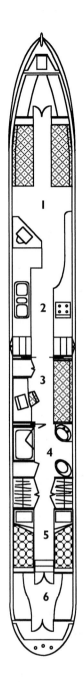

Rose was designed by its owner, a design engineer, to satisfy a number of specific requirements. The basic need was for a two-person boat that could also accommodate visiting family and friends without difficulty. It was to be open in character, have no wasted space and allow the owner's large physique to move around it without having to stoop or bend.

He tried at first to squeeze all these requirements into 57ft 6in but soon found that it was impossible. Having breached the go-anywhere barrier, he decided to plan the boat from the inside out and see how it developed. The result is a 67ft boat.

To meet his requirements for openness and easy access, the owner decided to use a feature almost unique in modern private boats – a central corridor through the entire layout. This allows him to see from one end to the other and, being in the centre of the plan, the corridor benefits from the maximum headroom available and is not restricted by the inward slope of the cabin side.

Most of the areas found on a narrowboat can accommodate a central corridor without too much difficulty but the one which causes the greatest problems is the double bedroom. Here, the answer is to have two single beds, one on either side, and to mount these on rollers so that they can be slid towards one another to form a double bed when required. This might have been done manually but, being a design engineer, the owner could not resist installing electric motors.

Two 3ft wardrobes separate the bedroom from the walk-through bathroom, which has a toilet and vanity unit to one side and a shower to the other. To give sufficient headroom on the shower compartment, the tray is lowered so that the rim is level with the cabin floor, requiring a special drainage outlet to be manufactured. Another pet hate of the owner is doors that get in the way when they stand open so there is no door to divide the bathroom from the bedroom and a sliding door which disappears out of sight where the bathroom meets the next space which is a small study.

Shell built by G & J Reeves (01926 815581)
Fitted out by Warwickshire Narrowboats (01788 832449)

1 Saloon	13ft 0in
2 Galley	10 ft 0in
3 Study	7 ft 0in
4 Bathroom	6 ft 0in
5 Bedroom	10 ft 0in
6 Rear deck	6ft 0in

Full review in
Waterways World
January 2001

Rose showing the cratch-covered front deck.

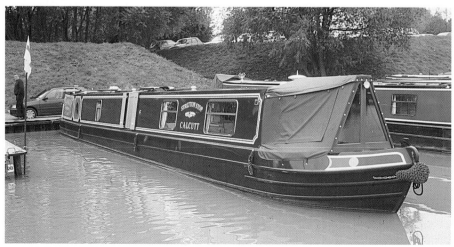

The study contains a desk along one side and a fixed seat that converts to a single bed on the other. Another pair of sliding doors leads to the galley. Here, the corridor takes the slightest of detours around the base of the L-shaped worktop but this projects only to the centre line of the boat and not two-thirds of the way across as is more usual.

The saloon has two opposed benches that convert to single beds by pulling them away from the cabin side to give more shoulder room. This feature can also be used to adjust the rake of the seat back. Finally, the front deck has a lower-than-normal floor level so that it feels more like an extension to the saloon.

Rose breaks several of the accepted rules of narrowboat layouts but it has been done in such an assured way that the result is a very pleasant cruising boat.

Top (right): Contrasting desk in the study.

Left: The centre corridor takes a slight detour in the galley.

Right: Two single beds convert to … one double bed.

Bottom (left): Fixed seating in the saloon converts to beds.

Bottom (right): The front deck is lowered to give standing headroom.

Charis

A 70ft semi-traditional narrowboat designed as a luxury hire boat

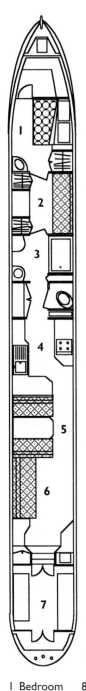

Charis was built partly for the owners' use but it was also intended to be used as a luxury hire boat. For this reason, it has many features that are not normally seen on a private boat and these demonstrate what is possible if you look at a subject from a different point of view.

The rear deck is semi-traditional and is large enough to seat six people in comfort around a folding table. Moving inside through the centrally placed double doors and down the fixed steps, there is a large day area comprising the saloon and dinette. Either side of the rear doors are angled cabinets and, let into a recess in the rear bulkhead is a flat screen television. Seating consists of a fixed bench that converts to one lengthways double or two single beds. The dinette goes further by converting to either a 4ft double, a 6ft cross bed or two 2ft singles and a cot. In day mode, it can seat up to eight people.

The large L-shaped galley moves the corridor back into the centre of the plan where it remains throughout the rest of the layout. There is a refuge area for the cook in the crook of the 'L' and the corridor widens towards the front, which creates another passing place for the crew. The galley is equipped with every piece of equipment you would expect to find in a domestic kitchen, including a dishwasher.

Next comes an enclosed toilet compartment on one side of the corridor and a full height cupboard on the other. A through bathroom follows with a large shower cubicle and vanity unit-cum-dressing table.

You then arrive in the intriguingly named 'relaxation' cabin which, if the boat is generously occupied, could contain one or two single bunks or, with a smaller complement, could become a dressing area, a study or – a relaxation cabin.

Shell built by G & J Reeves (01926 815581)
Fit out by Kingsground Narrowboats (01869 233444)

Charis showing the long semi-traditional rear deck.

1 Bedroom	8ft 0in
2 Relaxation cabin	6ft 6in
3 Bathroom	8ft 0in
4 Galley	9ft 0in
5 Dinette	6ft 6in
6 Saloon	14ft 0in
7 Rear deck	7ft 0in

Full review in
Waterways World
October 2001

Finally, there is the main bedroom with a thwartships double bed. This is partly demountable to give access to the front deck via a door located on the port side. The front deck is protected by a cratch and covers, and contains an L-shaped fixed seat and space for a small table.

On a boat with a semi-traditional or cruiser stern, it makes good sense to locate the saloon at the rear of the cabin but it is a shame that there is no window in the rear bulkhead or doors to give a permanent visual link from inside to outside. It is also surprising that a boat designed to give up to eight people a high quality cruising experience has only one toilet. Transposing the relaxation room and bathroom, and adding a small toilet compartment towards the rear of the boat would have given greater privacy at night.

Above: The dinette converts to several combinations of beds.

Left: Stylish joinery in the through bathroom.

Right: Two bunks in the 'relaxation' cabin.

Right: The thwartships double bed pulled back to allow access to the front deck.

Bottom (left): The galley looking towards the bathroom.

Bottom (right): Steps lead from the saloon to the rear deck.

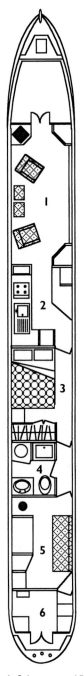

Nerissa

A 70ft traditional-style narrowboat with a novel rear deck and an unconventional boatman's cabin

Nerissa is a full-length boat designed for extended cruising. The main areas of accommodation, although relatively conventionally planned, are generously sized and well detailed. However, there are two features towards the rear that are more innovative.

The engine room is at the rear and is entered via a pair of doors and a very large rear sliding hatch. When opened fully, this creates a semi-traditional deck but, when closed, gives the enclosure and security of a traditional stern. A small flap in the rear edge of the hatch would have allowed the steerer even greater weather protection while cruising. The area beneath the hatch contains the instruments and controls and an inverter/charger. Under the floorboards are the central heating boiler, the battery bank and the cocooned engine.

Moving forward, there is day-cum-guest cabin that has most of the elements of a boatman's cabin but with some subtle twists. Both entry and exit doors are to the starboard side rather than being centrally placed and the diesel stove, which replaces the coal-fired range, is towards the front and not the rear of the cabin. Nevertheless, the arch topped table cupboard and drop down 'bed'ole' with their scumble finish and rose decorated panels give a decidedly traditional feel to this part of the boat.

Next is the bathroom, which has a shower and airing cupboard. This is followed by the main bedroom where the woodwork, as in the remainder of the boat, is in maple and cherry.

In the galley, the gas hob and oven, microwave, sink unit and washer drier are incorporated into custom-built units including a wall-mounted plate rack. The division between the galley and the saloon is marked by two interesting features. On the port side, there is a

Shell built by Mel Davis (01623 748592)
Fitted out by Nimbus Narrowboats (0116 269 3069)

The long front deck balances the cabin in this full-length boat.

1 Saloon	15ft 0in
2 Galley	9ft 0in
3 Bedroom	10ft 0in
4 Bathroom	6ft 0in
5 Day cabin	10ft 0in
6 Engine	
room	5ft 0in

Full review in
Waterways World
September 2002

cabinet with glazed doors, supported by two timber columns that gives a good degree of separation between the two spaces. On the other side, is an angled, full height cupboard with arch-topped doors, reminiscent of the one in the boatman's cabin but made of solid hardwood with plenty of elaborate mouldings.

At the front end of the saloon is a similar cabinet containing the TV and hi-fi and, in between these, is a range of under-gunwale units with hinged panels that can be raised to become useful tables and shelves. Another diesel-fired stove is on the opposite side of the front doors and seating is provided by two reclining chairs and stools.

The 7ft front deck is built over the water tank and a tank for the diesel stove and there are doors that give access to the two weed hatches for the bow thruster propellers. Taken with the 5ft foredeck, this may seem rather generous but, quite apart from the useful outdoor space it provides, anything less would look out of proportion on a 70ft boat.

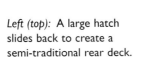

Left (top): A large hatch slides back to create a semi-traditional rear deck.

Left (middle): Traditional details and scumble in the rear day cabin.

Left (bottom): Conventional planning in the bathroom.

Right (top): Attractive wardrobe and dressing table in the bedroom.

Right (middle): Spacious and airy saloon.

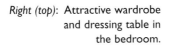

Right (bottom): All mod cons in the L-shaped galley.

Appendix A

Narrowboat Shell Builders
Shell builders who do not normally fit out but may be able to recommend a boatfitter

Derbyshire
Cuttwater Boats
48 Storforth Lane Trading Estate
Hasland
Chesterfield
Derbyshire
S41 0QR
01246 555562

Essex
Grant & Livingston Ltd
Kings Road
Charfleets Industrial Estate
Canvey Island
Essex
SS8 0RA
01268 696855
www,grantandlivingstonltd.com

Leicestershire
HT Fabrications Ltd
420 Thurnaston Boulvevard
Leicester
LE4 7LE
0116 2761814

Northamptonshire
Ivybridge Marine Ltd
Station House
Station Road
Watford
Northamptonshire
NN6 7UL
01327 704847

Nottinghamshire
Mel Davis Boatbuilders
Norwood Farm
Langwith
Mansfield
Nottinghamshire
NG20 9JA
01623 748592
www.meldavis.com

P.J. Barber Boatbuilders Ltd
Sheet Stores Basin
Sheet Stores Industrial Estate
Long Eaton
Nottingham
NG10 1AU
0115 9461752

Langley Mill Boatyard
Derby Road
Langley Mill
Nottingham
NG16 4AA
01773 760758

Paul Widdowson Boats
Unit 166 Road D
Boughton Industrial Estate
New Ollerton
Near Newark
Nottinghamshire
NG22 9LE
01623 835 777

Shropshire
David Harris Boatbuilders
27 Blakeway Close
Broseley
Shropshire
TF12 5SS
01952 882 468 / 07950 097 788

Price, Fallows
Ennerdale Road
Harlescott Industrial Estate
Shrewsbury
SY1 3LD
01743 448344

John South Boats
89 Condover Industrial Estate
Dorrington
Shropshire
SY5 7NH
01743 718415

Staffordshire
Burton Narrowboats Ltd
63a Queens Street
Burton-on-Trent
Staffordshire
DE14 3LW
07971 186408 / 07970 885231

CM Boat Builders Ltd
21 Wilks Wood
Cresswell
Stafford
ST18 9QR
01785 251 221

Canalcraft (Boatbuilders) Ltd
The Wharf
Watling Street
Gailey
Staffordshire
ST19 5PR
01902 791811
www.jdboats.co.uk

Heywood Boatbuilders
117 Pennyfields Rd
Newchapel
Kidsgrove
Stoke on Trent
Staffordshire
ST7 4PS
07968 508529

Tim Tyler Boatbuilders Ltd
New Road Industrial Estate
New Road
Hixon
Staffordshire
ST18 0PJ
01889 271414

Warwickshire
Bluewater Boats
12 Manor Road
Harbury
Leamington Spa
Warwickshire
CV33 9HY
01926 811699
www.bluewaterboats.co.uk

G&J Reeves Boatbuilders
Coventry Bridge Yard
Tomlow Road
Napton-on-the-Hill
Napton
Warwickshire
CV47 8HX
01926 815581

Pro-Build Narrowboats Ltd
Stockton Hill Farm
Stockton
Southam
Warkwickshire
CV47 8HS
01926 815998

West Midlands
Mercia Canal Boats Ltd
Units K1 & K3
Dudley Central Trading Estate
Shaw Road
Dudley
West Midlands
DY2 8QX
01384 456 678
www.merciacanalboats.co.uk

The Sterling Boat Company
Baker House
Hayes
Lye
Stourbridge
West Midlands
DY9 8RS
01384 422 291 / 424 232
www.sterlingboatco.com

Worcestershire

Alexander Boatbuilders
Unit 1A
Chadwick Bank Ind Est
Stourport-on-Severn
Worcestershire
DY13 9OW
01299 251471

Yorkshire – South

Eastwood Engineering
West Stockwith Industrial Park
Stockwith Road
Misterton
Doncaster
South Yorkshire
DN10 4ES
07739 346 343
www.eastwood-boats.co.uk

French & Peel Boatbuilders
Staniland Marina
Lock Hill
Thorne
South Yorkshire
DN8 5EP
01405 817954

Jonathan Wilson Boatbuilders
Victoria Boatyard
Sussex Street
Sheffield
S4 7YY
0114 278 1234

Yorkshire – West

Tayberg Steel Boats
Brookfoot Mills
Elland Road
Brighouse
West Yorkshire
HD6 2QS
01484 400221

This information is from the *Waterways World Annual 2005*. Up-to-date names, addresses and contact infomation will be found in the current edition of the *Waterways World Annual*, published in March each year and available from newsagents and from boatyards and marinas around the canal system

Appendix B

Narrowboat Builders
(see Appendix A for Narrowboat Shell Builders)

ENGLAND & WALES
Avon
R.L.L. Boats
Unit 1 Broadmead Industrial Estate
Broadmead Lane
Keynsham
Bristol
BS31 1ST
01179 869860
www.rllboats.co.uk

Bedfordshire
Grebe Canal Cruises
Pitstone Wharf
Pitstone
Leighton Buzzard
Bedfordshire
LU7 9AD
01296 661920

Havencraft Boats Ltd
Unit 7
44-46 Bunyan Road
Kempston
Bedford
MK42 8HL
01234 841 651 / 07710 140 640
www.russhubbleboats.co.uk

Lockhart Plant-Marine Ltd
Milton Keynes Marina
Peartree Bridge
Milton Keynes
MK6 3BX
01908 672672

Wyvern Shipping Co
Rothschild Road
Linslade
Leighton Buzzard
Bedfordshire
LU7 2TF
01525 372355
www.canalholidays.co.uk

Berkshire
Reading Marine
Aldermaston Wharf
Padworth
Reading
RG7 4JS
0118 971 3666

Buckinghamshire
High Line Yachting Ltd
Mansion Lane
Iver
Buckinghamshire
SL0 9RG
01753 651496
www.high-line.co.uk

Cambridgeshire
Eastern Caravans & Narrowboats
Newark Road Industrial Estate
Peterborough
Cambridgeshire
PE1 5YD
01733 310083

Fox Narrowboats Ltd
10 Marina Drive
March
Cambridgeshire
PE15 0AU
01354 652770
www.foxboats.co.uk

Hartford Marina
Banks End
Huntingdon
Cambridgeshire
PE28 2AA
01480 454677

Keith Wood Narrowboats Ltd
Lime Kiln Industrial Estate
Lime Kiln Lane
Stilton
Peterborough
Cambridgeshire
PE7 3SA
01733 242786
www.canalboatbuilders.com

Westview Marine Services
Earith
High Street
Huntingdon
Cambridgeshire
PE28 3PN
01487 840414
www.westviewmarineservices.co.uk

Cheshire
Boat Building Services
Unit 2
Indigo Road Business Park
Ellesmere Port
Cheshire
CH65 4AJ
0151 357 1949

Braidbar Boats
Lord Vernon's Wharf
Lyme Road
Higher Poynton
Cheshire
SK12 1TH
01625 873471
www.braidbarboats.co.uk

Cheshire Narrowboats
c/o Lymm Marina

Warrington Lane
Lymm
Cheshire
WA13 0SW
01925 752 945
www.lmbs.co.uk

Claymoore Navigation
The Wharf
Preston Brook
Warrington
Cheshire
WA4 4BA
01928 717273
www.claymoore.co.uk

DBE Boat Construction
1 Sandy Lane
Boughton
Chester
CH3 5UL
01244 540400/07891 091556

Elton Moss Boatbuilders
Elton Moss Canal Bridge
Elworth
Sandbach
Cheshire
CW11 3PW
01270 760 770
www.eltonmossboats.com

Kings Lock Chandlery
Boothe Lane
Middlewich
Cheshire
CW10 0JJ
01606 737564

Lees Narrowboats
Warble Wharf
Broadway
Hyde
Cheshire
SK14 4QF
0161 367 9205 / 07799 533 072
www.leesnarrowboats..co.uk

Middlewich Narrowboats
Canal Terrace
Middlewich
Cheshire
CW10 9BD
01606 832 460
www.middlewichboats.co.uk

Midway Boats Ltd - Barbridge Marina
Barbridge Junction
Wardle
Nantwich
Cheshire
CW5 6BE
01270 528482

Navigation Narrowboats
Basin End
Chester Road
Nantwich
Cheshire
CW5 8LB
01270 625122
www.nantwichcanalcentre.co.uk

Northern Marine Services
The Old Camp Shop
Warrington Lane
Lymm
Cheshire
WA13 0SW
01925 756285
www.northernboats.co.uk

Northwich Boat Company
Elton Moss Canal Bridge
Elworth
Sandbach
Cheshire
CW11 3PW
01270 760 770
www.thenorthwichboat.com

Olympus Narrowboats
Wincham Wharf
220 Manchester Road
Lostock Gralam
Northwich
Cheshire
CW9 7NT
01606 43048

Orchard Marina Ltd
School Road
Rud Heath
Northwich
Cheshire
CW9 7RG
01606 42082
www.orchardmarina.co.uk

Warble Narrowboats
Warble Wharf
Broadway
Hyde
Nr Stockport
Cheshire
SK14 4QF
0161 367 9205 / 07799 533072
www.leesnarrowboats.co.uk

Cleveland
HQ Engineering Ltd
Burn Road
Hartlepool
TS25 1PL
01429 276 551 / 01924 384 981 (sales)
www.hqengineering.com

County Durham
South West Durham Steelcraft Ltd
Old Colliery Buildings
Trimdon Grange Industrial Estate
Trimdon Grange
County Durham

TS29 6PA
01429 881300
www.swdsteelcraft.com

Derbyshire
Dale Leisure Marine
Unit 47, Avenue 3
Storforth Trading Estate
Hasland
Chesterfield
S41 0QR
01246 235599

Dobsons Wharf Boats Ltd
Dobsons Wharf
Shardlow
Derbyshire
DE72 2GJ
01332 792271

MCC Stenson Boatbuilders
Stenson Marina
Stenson
Derby
DE73 1HL
01283 701933
www.mccboats.co.uk

Measham Boats Ltd
Mannings Terrace
Measham
Swadlincote
DE12 7HU
01530 274301

New Mills Marina Ltd
Hibbert Street
New Mills
High Peak
SK22 3JJ
01663 741310
www.newmillsmarina.com

Paul David Westby Boatbuilders
Kegworth Marine
Kingston Lane
Kegworth
Derby
DE74 2FS
01509 6723004

Ricochet
Shardlow Marina
London Road
Shardlow
Derby
DE27 2GL
01332 799966

Sea Otter Boats
Adelphi Way
Ireland Industrial Estate
Staveley
Chesterfield
S43 3LS
01246 470005
www.seaotterboats.co.uk

Gloucestershire
R.W. Davis & Son Ltd
Junction Dry Dock
Saul
Gloucester
GL2 7LA
01452 740233
www.rwdavis.co.uk

Simpson Boats Ltd
23 Dock Road
Sharpness
Gloucestershire
GL13 9UA
01453 811247
www.simpsonboats.co.uk

Lancashire
Brayzel Narrowboats
Bridge House Marina
Nateby Crossing Lane
Nateby
Preston
Lancashire
PR3 0JJ
01995 601515
www.brayzelnarrowboats.co.uk

Classic Narrowboats Ltd
Wheelton Boatyard
Kenyon Lane
Wheelton
Chorley
Lancashire
PR6 8EX
01254 831444

Douglas Marine Ltd
Douglas Boatyard
Becconsall Lane
Hesketh Bank
Preston
Lancashire
PR4 6RR
01772 812462
www.douglas-marine.co.uk

DualDuel Narrowboats
Unit A
Alpha Fry Building
Mayfield St
Rochdale
Lancashire
OL16 2NM
01706 712942/07703 577757

Dursley & Hurst Narrowboats Ltd
Unit B 5 (4)
Moss Industrial Estate
St Helens Road
Leigh
Lancashire
WN7 3PT
01942 675 552
www.boatfitters.co.uk

Lower Park Marina
Kelbrook Road
Barnoldswick

Lancashire
BB18 5TB
01282 815883
www.pendletourism.com

Pickwell & Arnold
Unit 10
Nanholme Mill
Shaw Wood Road
Todmorden
Lancashire
OL14 6DA
01706 812411

Leicestershire
Fosse Marine ltd
Regent House
Regent Road
Countesthorpe
Leicestershire
LE8 5RF
0116 277 5000
www.fossemarine.com

Riverview Narrowboats
120 Station Road
Kegworth
Leicestershire
DE74 2FR
01509 672084

Lincolnshire
Fernwood Craft
Unit 2C
Sewstern Industrial Estate
Sewstern
Grantham
Lincolnshire
NG33 5RD
01476 860440
www.fernwoodcraft.co.uk

George Blades Narrowboats
Unit 2
Main Road
Wrangle
Boston
Lincolnshire
PE22 9AZ
01205 871429

Witham Narrowboats Ltd
Red House Farm
Thorpe Road
Whisby
Lincoln
LN6 9BT
07790 381859

Manchester
Bridgewater Boatbuilders
Garden Lane
Boothstown
Worsley
Manchester
M28 1JX
0161 7908144

Crown Narrowboats Ltd
80 Rocky Lane
Monton
Eccles
Manchester
M30 9LY
0161 7070087
www.crownnarrowboats.co.uk

Sabre Narrowboats Ltd
Unit 1A
Barton Business Park
Cawdor Street
Manchester
M30 0QF
0161 789 3023

Triton Boatfitters
3 Eliza Anne Street
Patricroft
Eccles
Manchester
M30 0GL
0161 787 9200
www.tritonboatfitters.co.uk

Merseyside
Amberdale Boats
10-12 Forth Street
Bankhall
Liverpool
L20 8JS
0151 933 3113
www.amberdaleboats.co.uk

John White Boatbuilders
Unit 17A
Weaver Industrial Estate
Blackburn Street
Garston
Merseyside
L19 8JA
0151 4277282
www.canaljunction.com

Liverpool Boat Co Ltd
25-29 Sefton Street
Liverpool
L8 5SL
0151 707 0722
www.liverpoolboatco.co.uk

RW Boatbuilders
62 Old Bidston Road
Birkenhead
Merseyside
CH41 8BL
0151 653 4597
www.rwboatbuilders.com

Middlesex
High Line Yachting Ltd
Packet Boat Marina
Cowley Peachey
Middlesex
UB8 2JS
01895 442644
www.high-line.co.uk

Hilston and Neal
Constables Boathouse
5–17 Thames Street
Hampton
Middlesex
TW12 2EW
020 89794818 / 01372 743 418

Otter Marine Services
Unit 3
Platt's Eyot
Lower Sunbury Road
Middlesex
TW12 2HF
020 89419636
www.ottermarine.co.uk

Thanetcraft Ltd
29 Popes Grove
Strawberry Hill
Twickenham
Middlesex
TW1 4JZ
020 8894 5218
www.thanetcraft.com

Northamptonshire
Baxter Boatfitting Services
The Wharf
Yardley Gobion
Northamptonshire
NN12 7UE
01908 542 844
www.baxterboatfittingservices.co.uk

C&G Narrowboats
The Boatshed
Crick Wharf
West Haddon Road
Crick
Northamptonshire
NN6 7XT
01788 822275
www.narrowboatfitters.com

D.B. Boatfitting Ltd
The Wharf
Braunston Marina
Braunston
Nr Daventry
Northamptonshire
NN11 7JH
01788 891727
www.dbboatfitting.co.uk

Dave Thomas
The Trade Centre, Unit 2
Braunston Marina
Braunston
Nr Daventry
Northamptonshire
NN11 7JH
01788 891181

Merlin Narrowboats Ltd
Braunston Marina
Braunston
Nr Daventry
Northamptonshire

NN11 7JH
01788 891750
www.merlinnarrowboats.com

Milburn Boats
Bridge Grounds
Staverton
Nr Daventry
Northamptonshire
NN11 6BG
01327 702164

Stowe Hill Marine Ltd
Stowe Hill Wharf
Weedon
Northamptonshire
NN7 4RZ
01327 341365
www.stowehill.com

Weltonfield Narrowboats Ltd
Welton Hythe
Daventry
Northamptonshire
NN11 5LG
01327 842282
www.weltonfield.co.uk

Wharf House Narrowboats Ltd
Braunston Bottom Lock
Braunston
Northamptonshire
NN11 7HJ
01788 899041

Nottinghamshire
C & N Narrowboats
13 Hillside Drive
Long Eaton
Nottinghamshire
NG10 4AH
01452 725362

Castle Boatbuilders
22 Kilton Terrace
Worksop
Nottinghamshire
S80 2DQ
01909 478250

Jenny Wren Narrow Boats
159 Boughton Industrial Estate
Boughton
Newark
Nottinghamshire
NG22 9LD
07830 366 859

Perkins Narrowboats Ltd
34 Spinney Close
West Bridgford
Nottingham
NG2 6HH
0115 923 1210
www.perkinsnarrowboats.co.uk

Redhill Marina
Ratcliffe-on-Soar
Nottingham

NG11 0EB
01509 672770
www.redhill-marina.co.uk

Oxfordshire
Aynho Dock Services
Canal Wharf
Aynho
Nr Banbury
Oxfordshire
OX17 3BP
01869 338483

Heyford Wharf Ltd
Canal Wharf
Station Road
Lower Heyford
Bicester
Oxfordshire
OX25 5PD
01869 340348

Kingsground Narrowboats
Building 103
Heyford Business Park
Upper Heyford
Bicester
Oxfordshire
OX25 5HA
01869 233444
www.kingsground.co.uk

Michael Walker Narrowboats
5 The Paddocks
Souldern
Bicester
Oxfordshire
OX27 7LG
01869 345 291

N T Boats Ltd
Heyford Wharf
Lower Heyford
Oxfordshire
OX25 5PD
01869 321141

Nomad Narrowboats
Unit 1
Brymbo Road
Hook Norton
Oxfordshire
OX15 5LS
01608 730 808

Oxford Cruisers
The Boat Centre
Eynsham
Oxfordshire
OX29 10A
01865 881698

Walker Services Narrowboats
5 The Paddocks
Souldern
Bicester
Oxforshire
OX27 7LG
01869 345291/07798 533303

Powys
Cambrian Cruisers
Pencelli
Brecon
Powys
LD3 7LJ
01874 665315

Shropshire
Bettisfield Boats
The Moorings
Canalside
Bettisfield
Whitchurch
Shropshire
SY13 2LJ
01948 710465

Maesbury Marine Services
Maesbury Hall Mill
Morton
Nr. Oswestry
Shropshire
SY10 8BB
01691 676137
www.maesburymarineservices.co.uk

Maestermyn Marine
Ellesmere Road
Whittington
Oswestry
Shropshire
SY11 4NU
01691 662424

Whixall Marina Shropshire Ltd
Alders Lane
Whixall
Shropshire
SY13 2QP
01948 880540
www.whixallmarine.co.uk

Somerset
Andrew Moore Boats Ltd
Chilton Cantelo
Near Yeovil
Somerset
BA22 8BQ
07815 916 959
www.andrewmooreboats.com

Staffordshire
Countrywide Cruisers
The Wharf
Brewood
Staffordshire
ST19 9BG
01902 850166

Engineering & Canal Services
The Workshops
Hoo Mill Lock
Great Haywood
Staffordshire
ST18 0RG
01889 882 611

Narrowboat Planning

Harvey's Joinery
The Workshop
Wilnecote Lane
Belgrave
Tamworth
Staffordshire
B77 2LE
01827 250900/07971 977380
www.harveysboatbuilders.com

J.D. Boat Services
The Wharf
Watling Street
Gailey
Staffordshire
ST19 5PR
01902 791811
www.jdboats.co.uk

Jannel Cruisers
Shobnall Marina
Shobnall Road
Burton-on-Trent
Staffordshire
DE14 2AU
01283 542718
www.jannel.co.uk

MGM Boats
Guildwell Canal Basin
Horninglow Road
Burton-on-Trent
Staffordshire
DE13 0SL
01283 561114
www.mgmboats.co.uk

MPS Narrowboats
Unit 1 Gibbs
Leafows Farm
Stafford Rd
Uttoxeter
Staffordshire
ST14 8QA
01889 567036/07729 363205

Piper Boats
PWS Industrial Estate
Tunstall Road
Biddulph
Stoke-on-Trent
ST8 7BE
01782 510610
www.piperboats.com

Roger Fuller (Boatbuilder) Ltd
Navigation House
1 Whitebridge Lane
Stone
Staffordshire
ST15 8LQ
01785 817506
www.canalnarrowboats.com

S.M. Hudson Boatbuilders
Glascote Basin Boatyard
Basin Lane
Glascote
Tamworth
Staffordshire

B77 2AH
01827 311317

Stoke-on-Trent Boatbuilding
Longport Wharf
Longport
Stoke-on-Trent
ST6 4NA
01782 813831

Stone Boatbuilding Co Ltd
Newcastle Road
Stone
Staffordshire
ST15 8JZ
01785 812688
www.stoneboatbuilding.co.uk

Streethay Wharf
Streethay
Lichfield
Staffordshire
WS13 8RJ
01543 414808
www.streethaywharf.co.uk

Swan Line Cruisers Ltd
Fradley Junction
Alrewas
Burton-on-Trent
Staffordshire
DE13 7DN
01283 790332

Teddesley Boat Co
Park Gate Lock
Teddesley Road
Penkridge
Staffordshire
ST19 5RH
01785 714692
www.narrowboats.co.uk

Whisky Boats Ltd
The Wharf
Norbury Junction
Norbury
Staffordshire
ST20 0PN
07802 409693

Warwickshire

Ashby Boat Company
Canal Wharf
Station Road
Stoke Golding
Nuneaton
Warwickshire
CV13 6EY
01455 212671
www.ashbyboats.co.uk

Ashby Boatbuilders
Ashby Canal Centre
Willow Park
Stoke Golding
Nuneaton
Warwickshire
CV13 6EU
01455 212636

Barry Hawkins Narrowboats Ltd
Baddesley Wharf
Holly Lane
Atherstone
Warwickshire
CV9 2EH
01827 711762
www.barryhawkins-narrowboats.com

Blue Haven Marine
Hillmorton Wharf
Crick Road
Rugby
Warwickshire
CV21 4PW
01788 540149

Brinklow Boat Services
The Wharf
Stretton under Fosse
Rugby
Warwickshire
CV23 0PR
01788 833331

Calcutt Boats Ltd
Calcutt Top Lock
Tomlow Road
Stockton
Southam
Warwickshire
CV47 8HX
01926 813757
www.calcuttboats.com

Central Craft Works Ltd
Old Barn Farm
Ladbrooke
Nr Southam
Warwickshire
CV47 0BD
01926 812218

Clifton Cruisers
Clifton Wharf
Vicarage Hill
Clifton-on-Dunsmore
Rugby
Warwickshire
CV23 0DG
01788 543570
www.cliftoncruisers.com

Colecraft Engineering
Southam Road
Long Itchington
Southam
Warwickshire
CV47 9QL
01926 814081
www.colecraft.co.uk

Delta Marine European Ltd
Nelson Wharf
Nelson Lane
Warwick
CV34 5JB
01926 499337
www.delta-marineservices.co.uk

Kate Boats
The Boatyard
Nelson Lane
Warwick
CV34 5JB
01926 492968
www.kateboats.com

Napton Marina Boatbuilding
Napton Marina
Stockton
Southam
Warwickshire
CV47 8HX
01926 813 644
www.napton-marina.co.uk

Stockton Dry Dock Co
Shop Lock Cottage
Stockton
Nr Southam
Warwickshire
CV47 8LD
01926 812093

Warwickshire Narrowboats
Fosseway
Stretton under Fosse
Rugby
Warwickshire
CV23 0PU
01788 832449

West Midlands
Alvechurch Boat Centres
Scarfield Wharf
Alvechurch
Birmingham
B48 7SQ
0121 445 2909
www.alvechurch.com

Associated Cruisers
Off Little Lane
Lock Street
Wolverhampton
WV1 1JJ
01902 423673

Barn Owl Narrowboats
232 Stanford Road
Brierley Hill
West Midlands
DY5 2QE
07981 214632/01384 348877

Black Country Narrowboats Ltd
Waterside Cottage
Prestwood Drive
Stourton
Stourbridge
West Midlands
DY7 5QT
01384 872135

Canal Transport Services Ltd
Norton Canes Dock
Lime Lane
Pelsall

Walsall
WS3 5AP
01543 374370

Darren Aldridge Boats
44 Preston Avenue
Sutton Coldfield
West Midlands
B76 1NZ
07870 400343
www.darrenaldridgeboats.co.uk

Grosvenor-Marsh Narrowboats Ltd
Unit 49A
Premier Business Park
Leys Road
Brierley Hill
West Midlands
DY5 3UP
07968 990 865

Ian Kemp Restoration Services
Dadfords Wharf
Bridge Street
Wordsley
Stourbridge
West Midlands
DY8 5YU
01384 485565

Lyons Boatyard
Canalside
Limekiln Lane
Warstock
Birmingham
B14 4SP
0121 474 4977

Norton Canes Boatbuilders
Norton Canes Docks
Lime Lane
Pelsall
Walsall
West Midlands
WS3 5AP
01543 374888

Orion Narrowboats
Ashwood Marina
Kingswinford
West Midlands
DY6 0AQ
01384 401464

Phil Jones
Hatherton Marina
Queens Road
Calf Heath
Wolverhampton
WV10 7DT
07831 153 028

Richard's Narrow Boats
85 West Ridge Road
Kings Heath
Birmingham
B13 0DZ
0121 777 0697
www.richardnarrowboats.com

Stephen Goldsbrough Boats
Knowle Hall Wharf
Kenilworth Road
Knowle
Solihull
West Midlands
B93 0JJ
01564 778210
www.sgboats.com

Wiltshire
Alvechurch Boat Centres
Hilperton Marina
Hammond Way
Trowbridge
Wiltshire
BA14 8RS
01225 769847 / 765243
www.alvechurch.com

Devizes Narrowboat Builders
Lower Foxhangers Farm
Rowde
Devizes
Wiltshire
SN10 1SS
01380 828848

M & P Steelcraft Ltd
Marsh Farm
Marsh Road
Hilperton
Trowbridge
Wiltshire
BA14 7PJ
01225 775100
www.mp-steelcraft.co.uk

Worcestershire
Aqualine
The New Boat Co
Hanbury Wharf
Droitwich
Worcestershire
WR9 7DU
01905 771 018
www.thenewboat.co.uk

Heritage Boatbuilders
Evesham Marina
Kings Road
Evesham
Worcestershire
WR11 5BU
01386 48882

J.L. Pinder & Sons (Trading as
Crafted Boats Ltd)
Unit 8–11
138 Hanbury Road
Stoke Prior
Bromsgrove
Worcestershire
B60 4JZ
01527 876438
www.jlpinderandsons.co.uk

Appendix B

Sandhills Narrowboats Ltd
Sandhills Farm
Edgioake Lane
Astwood Bank
Nr Redditch
Worcestershire
B96 6BG
01527 894409
www.sandhillsnarrowboats.co.uk

Severn Valley Boat Centre
Boat Shop
Mart Lane
Stourport-on-Severn
Worcestershire
DY13 9ER
01299 871165
www.severnboat.co.uk

Sirius Boatbuilders
Redstone Wharf
Sandy Lane
Stourport-on-Severn
Worcestershire
DY13 9QB
01299 871048
www.siriusyachts.com

Starline Marine
Upton Marina
Upton-on-Severn
Worcestershire
WR8 0PB
01684 574774
www.starlinemarine.co.uk

Stroudwater Cruisers
Engine Lane
Stourport-on-Severn
Worcestershire
DY13 9EP
01299 877222
www.stroudwater-cruisers.co.uk

Yorkshire

Blue Water Marina
Southend
Thorne
Yorkshire
DN8 5QR
01405 813165
www.bluewatermarina.co.uk

Fallwood Marina
Pollard Lane
Bramley
Leeds
LS13 1ER
0113 258 1074
www.fallwood-marina.co.uk

Selby Boat Centre
Bawtry Road
Selby
Yorkshire
YO8 8NB
0870 749 0061
www.selby-boat-centre.co.uk

Swiftcraft Moorings
Parkin Lane
Apperley Bridge
Bradford
Yorkshire
BD10 0NF
01274 611786

Yorkshire – South

Anthony M Cabinet Maker
Unit 9
Brunel Park
Blyth Road
Harworth
Doncaster
DN11 8NE
01302 751540 / 07941 816021
www.anthony-m.com

Louis & Joshua Boatbuilders
Thorne Marina
Hatfield Road
Thorne
Nr Doncaster
South Yorkshire
DN8 5RA
01405 814443
www.boatbuilders.org

Thorne Lock Marina Ltd (Staniland
Marine)
Loch Hill
Thorne
South Yorkshire
DN8 5EP
01405 813 150

Yorkshire Rose Marina
Unit 9
Leach Lane
Mexborough
South Yorkshire
S64 0EN
01709 571555

Yorkshire – West

Calder Valley Marine
Apperley Bridge Marina
Waterfront Mews
Apperley Bridge
West Yorkshire
BD10 0UR
01274 616 961
www.cvmarine.co.uk

Heron Boatbuilders Ltd
Junction 25 Business Park
Huddersfield Road
Mirfield
West Yorkshire
WF14 9DA
0500 585829

Ledgard Bridge Boat Co Ltd
Ledgard Wharf 29A
Butt End Mills
Mirfield
West Yorkshire
WF14 8PW
01924 491441
www.ledgardbridge-
boatcompany.com

Silsden Boats
Canal Wharf
Silsden
Keighley
West Yorkshire
BD20 0DE
01535 653675
www.silsdenboats.co.uk

Scotland

Corpach Boatbuilding Co Ltd
The Slipway
Corpach
Fort William
PH33 7NB
01397 772861
www.scottishboatyard.co.uk

This list is from the *Waterways World Annual 2005*. Up-to-date names, addresses and contact infomation will be found in the current edition of the *Waterways World Annual*, published in March each year and available from newsagents and from, boatyards and marinas around the canal system